The Big Slump

Zenith Books

Also in this series

The Big Slump

John Harris

illustrated with cartoons by
David Low

Zenith books
published by Hodder and Stoughton
in association with Hilary Rubinstein

Printed in Great Britain for Hodder and Stoughton Ltd.,
St. Paul's House, Warwick Lane, London, E.C.4, by
Cox & Wyman Ltd., London, Fakenham and Reading.

Contents

Contents

THEY had pale faces and soft, white, uncalloused hands. They stood on street corners for hours at a time, easily recognisable by their shabby clothes and the characteristic slouch which they had developed over the years. They had a general air of hopelessness about them. They were the workless.

Many of them were men who had once known pride in their crafts. Others were the unskilled who had been the first to lose their jobs. Yet others were the youngsters who had left school, grown up, married and had children of their own — and had never known what it was to work for their living. In 1933 there were almost 3,000,000 of them in Great Britain.

Outside the Labour Exchanges in the hard-hit North of England, there were long queues of such men. There were more queues outside the Public Assistance Offices, and outside any factory where it was rumoured there might be work the queues stretched for hundreds of yards.

Once these men had had a dignity. They had shaved carefully, put on their Sunday suits and collars and ties and held their heads high, expecting that they would be out of work for only a short time. But, as the days passed, and then the weeks and the months, and finally the years, their dignity had gone. The best suit had gone, too — pawned to raise money for the housekeeping. Heads were no longer held high and, through keeping their hands in their pockets and standing at street corners, they had developed the slouch that marked them all. Not only dignity had gone. Hope had gone, too.

Even the hands of their wives were harder than their own, because they at least had work to do; for the most part hard bitter work struggling to keep the family together and adequately fed, making do on too little of everything, altering clothes which had been acquired from charities, cutting them down and even remaking them to fit the children, searching the town for cheap vegetables, accepting any kind of menial task to help out the family fortunes and maintaining a secretive, almost conspiratorial, silence about it in case the authorities deducted the earnings from the charitable dole the husband drew.

In the factories and shipyards, the cranes were growing red with rust and grass was growing where thousands of feet had marched about their duties. And what was worse to the unemployed, after years of it nobody still really seemed to care. The attempts to help them appeared feeble, un-co-ordinated and uninspired and the efforts of politicians who had no great interest in their plight. The Government had run out of ideas. All the authorities could think of was to cut and cut and cut — dole, public assistance, every kind of relief.

In their homes, when they returned from the street corners where they spent their days, there was little to comfort them. There wasn't even the cheer of a radio because that had long since gone to the pawnshop. There probably wasn't even the ease of an arm-chair, because the Means Test, that evil inquisition into their ability to contribute to their own support, had insisted that everything that might realise money must be sold before relief could be given.

This was unemployment, and there were millions of unemployed. Britain was stagnating.

This was the Depression, the Slump as it was called, and

while the word "Slump" is usually applied to the period of the early thirties, in the worst-affected areas it seemed to stretch, with intervals of only comparative prosperity, from the end of the Great War of 1914–18 to Hitler's War of 1939. During the crisis years between 1929 — when there were already 1,250,000 men out of work — and 1931, when the Depression really hit England, another 1,500,000 lost their jobs. At the height of the slump, in January, 1933, the appalling total of 2,995,000 men — one out of every five in the working population — were without a job. Even in 1935, when the country had actually started to recover, in Jarrow alone eight out of every ten working men were unemployed. It was found by that time, in fact, that the whole thing had become a vicious circle, because the poverty created by unemployment was making men unemployable.

It was the grey period when whole areas of England turned their backs for ever on the Conservative Party and many men who had hitherto taken a middle-of-the-road view, were drawn to Communism; and when, on the Continent, the threat of anarchy that unemployment and poverty produced, brought about what many came to believe was the only answer — a Fascist authoritarian State, with a leader who could and did break away from all the old fetishes of established economics.

It seemed to stretch throughout the whole of the lives of the young men who were to fight and die in the Second World War. For many of them, only Hitler's threat to peace and the rearmament against him saved them from the humiliation of continued unemployment.

The Depression had its origin in a period of over-employment. The youngsters who have grown up since World War II in a similar period of prosperity in those once hard-hit areas, cannot conceive what those years of stagnation were like. But their fathers can. And, while these areas have changed and the conditions which existed then do not exist now, there is always at the back of the minds of those who do remember, when they read of Britain's economic state and the recessions artificially created by governments to stabilise the wobbling economy, the nagging thought – Could it happen again?

Two / The Top-Heavy Edifice

How did it start? Where did it start?

Without doubt the 1914–18 war, the cruellest and costliest that had ever been fought to that date, a world-shaking affair which had toppled dynasties and disrupted economic patterns across the whole globe, and the aftermath of that war, had had their effects; but the root of the trouble lay deeper.

There had been periods of bitterness and poverty before, but it was the Industrial Revolution which, transforming the whole structure of English society, changed these slumps from largely local affairs to more shattering periods when the nation as a whole was affected.

When George III came to the throne in 1760, Britain was mainly self-supporting and 90 per cent of the nation's food was provided by her own soil. Her clothes were nearly all spun and woven in cottage homes, and her iron was produced on a small scale by means of smelting with charcoal in the forested areas of the South and West. But gradually, over the next sixty years, England began to change from a rural community largely dependent on farming to an industrial community whose products and the growing wealth that came from those products helped her to play the major part in the long wars against Napoleon, not only with her own troops but with loans to other countries who might be persuaded to stand against the French tide. By 1820 she had become dependent on foreign trade for exports and imports; big farms were held by tenant-farmers who hired labourers; spinning and weaving were

being carried out in factories by paid "hands"; and iron
was being smelted by coal in great foundries in the North
and Midlands.

These developments came first in the Lancashire cotton
industry where Hargreaves's *Spinning Jenny*, Arkwright's
Water Frame and Crompton's *Mule* stepped up production.
One of the most successful lines which commerce took in
the eighteenth century was the export of rolls of cotton
cloth by ships' captains from British ports to West Africa;
there they were exchanged for Negro slaves who were
taken to the cotton plantations in America which in turn
produced the raw material for the Lancashire industry.

As the trade grew, men's minds began to work out ways
and means of increasing production. At this time, the only
transport from Manchester to the coast – apart from the
rough, rutted roads—was a canal originally built to transport coal. In an attempt to get their goods more quickly
to the ships at Liverpool, the Lancashire merchants com-
missioned the inventor of the new steam-drawn transport
in use from Stockton to Darlington, a self-taught Newcastle
collier called George Stephenson, to build the first passenger-
carrying railway across the damp South Lancashire plain. On
September 15, 1830, the line was opened by the great Duke
of Wellington, riding in a scarlet-bedecked carriage hauled
by one of Stephenson's steam-engines, *Northumbrian*.

The idea caught on, and within twenty years armies of
navvies had driven 5,000 miles of railway across Britain,
building viaducts across the valleys and tunnelling through
the hills. For the first time Britain's manufacturers were no
longer dependent on the indifferent roads and the slow
progress of horse-drawn transport.

The railways, as they grew, brought about the growth of
another industry. In twenty years, as the demands of the

railways made themselves felt, Britain's iron production soared from 1845 500,000 tons to 2,000,000 tons a year. (Between 1845 and 1847 8,500 miles of rail were sanctioned by Parliament and in five years of this great boom 1,500,000 tons of iron went on railway building alone.) Soon the manufacturers began to look round for new sources of ore. By the second half of the century, the old iron foundries had been overwhelmed by the vast new mills which had been built near the plentiful supplies in the Cleveland Hills, and Middlesbrough became the greatest of the ore-producing areas.

As the industry developed, so did the techniques, and when Henry Bessemer discovered in 1856 a cheap means of producing hardened steel, Sheffield took its place as the centre of the new manufacture. In thirty-five years it multiplied its steel output by fifty times, and furnaces ranged all the way from the town's eastern boundaries to the neighbouring towns of Rotherham and beyond.

It was natural at this time that the shipbuilders should turn to iron to build their vessels. By the mid-1850s, steam was as common as sail. The first steamship had been built in the eighteenth century and the first great iron steamship was launched in 1837. But the prejudice against the use of iron for ships remained until the iron-built *Great Britain*, launched in 1843, was wrecked in a gale in 1846; she remained aground for eleven months, in gale conditions which would have broken a wooden ship to pieces, but was eventually refloated and repaired without much difficulty. The reputation of the iron ship was made.

As the railway boom came to an end, the British shipmasters turned more and more to the building of these vast ships, and the boom returned to the point where it had begun – the ports. Britain had become an industrial nation. But she had been so busy with expansion and development that no one had noticed one dangerous tendency.

Largely through geographical circumstances such as the presence of coal or running water, industries had been concentrated into specific areas. Manchester, for instance, meant cotton. Bradford meant wool. Sheffield meant steel, South Wales meant coal. And in these areas there was little else. Their whole top-heavy economic edifice was built on these products.

*   *   *

Although there had been a severe slump in the cotton industry in the 1860s, during the American Civil War, when the ships of the Northern States had bottled up the South's cotton by their blockade, the industry began to boom again when peace returned across the Atlantic. And, as cotton thrived, so did all the other industries which had sprung from it. Newcastle, Gateshead and Darlington; Wigan, Bolton and Rochdale; Halifax, Huddersfield and Leeds; and Sheffield, Rotherham and Barnsley had become boom towns in which far-sighted men made fortunes.

The people of the North had turned with astonishing adaptability from the fields to the factories, and intelligent, energetic men who had been born in cottages had started small businesses and, in the boom years, had expanded them into vast empires. John Brown of Sheffield is a good example. A slater's son, he had been apprenticed to a firm which made cutlery and files. He had risen quickly to a partnership and, turning to the needs of the growing railways and with the profits from his invention of the conical steel buffer, he was able in 1854 to buy a works of his own in the Don Valley. Within thirty years, his factories covered twenty-five acres. The introduction of Henry Bessemer's steel-producing process soon enabled him to supply armour plating to most of Europe's naval powers.

Much of the finance for great enterprises of this kind had come from the fortunes of great landowners, but by this time the factories had grown so vast that even the enormous fortunes of these great families were no longer sufficient for the amount of expansion that was going on. And, as the South was inclined to regard the North as something of a savage land peopled by barbarians, the northern manufacturers turned towards their own moneylenders.

Unfortunately, however, to keep up with industry, towns were also building and expanding more than ever in their history, and eventually there simply wasn't the cash to pay for it all. The boom collapsed in 1866 when there was an immediate panic in London. Banks went out of business and several railways were bankrupted, and sterling was regarded with suspicion on the Continent for months.

It was almost a year before trade began to recover, but the boom was ended. The North had grown too fast and outrun its strength. It needed to reconsider and consolidate, and the acres of sooty bricks that had been thrown up around the factories were not to be changed for almost a hundred years. The industries had grown too big. The towns and cities themselves had grown too big. The populations had grown too big, and all those vast numbers of people who in the earlier part of the century had rushed to industry where they had seen the chance of making large sums of money were condemned to generations of living in a brick cage which had been built for them by speculators.

The conditions were frightful. As Disraeli wrote in 1845, England had become a country inhabited by two nations — the rich and the poor. The contrast between the wealth of the aristocracy and the middle classes and the abject poverty of the majority of the working classes was glaring.

Because there was no fast or cheap transport, the worker was obliged to live close to the factory where he worked. Disraeli has described in one of his novels the long lines of dingy tenements without public buildings, churches, institutes or theatres. There were only coarse and grimy shops and alleys streaming with filth, and courtyards where the absence of sanitation led to dreadful epidemics.

The overcrowding was appalling because the builders, without concern for sanitation or health, had spent as little as possible on housing the workers. Yet even the cheapest house could not be let at a rent commensurate with the wages paid, and all too often houses, sometimes even single rooms, were shared by several families.

There was no running water, chiefly because the growth of the towns had outstripped the supply, and what there was, was often polluted. The worst sanitary conditions existed, and Engels, co-founder with Marx of Communism, discovered in Manchester in 1844 that for every 120 persons only one privy was provided.

Although Poor Law Boards, Boards of Health and Royal Commissions undid a great deal of the damage in the latter part of the nineteenth century, by the beginning of the twentieth century, there were still many black spots in the industrial areas. New and better houses had been built, but all too often only the skilled artisan could afford to pay the rents and it was not until the principle of Government subsidies was accepted that the poorest worker could expect a decent home. Only a few far-sighted people like George Cadbury, a Quaker manufacturer who built a new factory in the countryside at Bournville, the soap firm of Lever Brothers, who established their new works at Port Sunlight on the Wirral in Cheshire and Ebenezer Howard, the founder of the garden city principle, realised that better conditions in the end produced better work. It was not until 1903 that a company promoted by Howard and his friends bought a rural site near Hitchin in Hertfordshire and began to build a garden city, Letchworth. The idea did not catch on, however, and by 1919, only one other such town, Welwyn, had been established.

For the most part the worker was condemned to the mean streets around the factory where he toiled all day, spending his leisure at the local pub, or on his Saturday afternoons watching his favourite football team. Once a year, in Wakes week, he would take his family to the seaside, occasionally for a few days but for the most part on a hectic day-trip. For the rest of the year, his life was dull, drab and bounded entirely by the horizon of the factory. There was a great deal of reason for the bitterness he often felt and which he was to experience in full measure in the years following the end of the Great War.

Three / The Unforgiving Victor

AMONG the indirect causes of the First World War was the vast nineteenth-century industrial organisation, the very thing which, paradoxically, it eventually destroyed. For most of the nineteenth century, Britain had been the most powerful and respected of the European nations, but Germany, starting later in the industrial race, had made great strides to catch her up. The sudden growth of confidence there, which sprang from the immense expansion of her industrial and commercial strength, had led her to a growing jealousy of Britain's strength and her industrial and commercial security. This, in turn, led an alarmed Britain into alliances and alignments against her.

When the spark was lit the colossal industrial output on both sides provoked the political and military leaders into anticipating a quick success. The vast armies, made possible by the colossal stores of arms that had been built up, began to move to their points of impact on the frontiers. But, once started, the war could not easily be stopped. Four years later, it had destroyed a whole generation.

Although Europe had been planning the war for years, its actual character came as a complete surprise. Generals trained in another century and in other tactics were incapable of dealing with the trench battles which were imposed upon them, and they exhausted their armies in vast futile attacks which did nothing but produce casualties. The total killed has been estimated to exceed 10,000,000, of which 1,000,000 came from the British Empire. France's losses were even higher while Germany's climbed up over the 2,000,000 mark. Among the killed were the best, the most intelligent and the most industrious of the world's young men who might well have lifted Europe from the stagnation that was to fall upon it in the years following the slaughter.

* * *

The world of 1918 was in nearly every sense different from that of 1914. It was shaken and weak and totally lacked that sense of stability, that belief in progress, which had been the hallmark of the late nineteenth century. The conflict had brought about the collapse of the great Austro – Hungarian, Russian and German Empires and laid burdens on countries which bore them to the ground. And it gave impulse to new political and social conceptions, particularly Communism, and a new attitude towards the relationship between owner and working man.

Together with the conditions imposed by the Versailles Peace Treaty of 1919, all these things provided the foundations for the depression which was to follow so quickly and destroy all those bright hopes that had sustained the troops through their four-year ordeal.

Thirty-seven Governments were represented at the peace conference but the real decisions were settled at the private meetings of the "Big Four" — President Wilson, of the United States; M. Clemenceau, of France; Prime Minister David Lloyd George, of Great Britain; and Signor Orlando, of Italy.

President Wilson had immense prestige in Europe, because of his lofty utterances on democracy and peace and because he controlled vast resources in the United States which were much less affected by the war than those of the rest of the world. But the dominant personality at the

Conference was without doubt Georges Eugène Benjamin
Clemenceau, known to the newspapers as "Tiger", a grim
unbending Frenchman who was rigidly determined that the
utmost advantage should be wrung from the victory to
ensure that Germany should never again be in a position to
invade French soil.

Born in 1841, he had been mayor of Montmartre during
the siege of Paris in the Franco – Prussian War of 1870. Later,
he became a deputy for Paris and his biting eloquence
marked him immediately. His gift, however, was not so
much in governing as in destroying Governments, which he
did one after another with his mordant wit and unflagging
energy. Before the war he led France as Premier for only
three years from 1906 to 1909, but in the war of 1914–18,
the grim old man had become an almost legendary figure as
the symbol of French resistance to the Germans. At the end,
having grasped the reins of office once more in 1917, he
emerged as an unforgiving victor.

At Versailles, while Wilson and Lloyd George were largely
concerned with removing the causes of friction between
European nations which had brought about the war,
Clemenceau, in his determination to safeguard France, per-
mitted no German objections to his wishes and insisted that
reparations, heavy reparations, were the only conditions he
would accept.

The Germans had hoped that by overthrowing the
Imperial family, the Hohenzollerns, and establishing a
republic, they would gain better terms from the victors but,
in fact, the terms could not have been more harsh. They had
to give Alsace-Lorraine, which they had annexed in 1870,
back to France, and corners were chipped off all round their
country to create buffer states as a preventive to war.
They were forced to admit their sole responsibility for the

war and were condemned to an indemnity so vast that the
amount could not easily be fixed — it had to be settled later
by a special commission. They were to surrender all their
war fleet and most of their merchant vessels; their future
army and navy were to be limited to the minimum necessary for defence, and they were forbidden to have submarines
or an air force. Finally, their colonies were taken from them,
to be governed and developed under the supervision of the
new League of Nations.

In these harsh conditions were all the seeds of another
conflict, and more than one forward-thinking economist
saw the danger. Among them was John Maynard Keynes,
later Lord Keynes and a figure of world importance, who
declared that the terms of the Versailles Treaty were ill-
conceived, vindictive and evil, and likely to prejudice world

January 7, 1929
Defeated Germany was saddled with enormous debts in the form of
reparations after World War I and then had to be granted loans to enable
her to pay them. The endless repayments embittered Germany who, when
the loans stopped after the Wall Street crash of 1929, collapsed too.
(Parker Gilbert was Agent-General for Reparation Payments.)

economy. Though his views probably put a weapon in the hands of the Nationalist movements in Germany in the thirties and may have increased the future isolationism of America, there is not much doubt but that he was right. His beliefs carried little weight at the time, however, and he resigned from his position on the British delegation to the peace conference.

The demands of Clemenceau prevailed and Germany was condemned to be roped and hog-tied, denied help yet prevented from helping herself. These conditions were not only to be among the causes of the world-wide slump that was to follow a decade later but also indirectly — by sowing the seeds of resentment which led to the Second World War — some of the reasons for its end.

Four / The Wasted Years

In one of his poems, T. S. Eliot refers to the twenty years between the Peace of Versailles and the outbreak of the Second World War as "the wasted years".

Hopes were high in 1919 that, after four years of war waged on an unprecedented scale, a new and better world was to emerge as a reward for the sacrifices which had been made. But the story of those twenty years turned out, in fact, to be very different indeed.

In 1919, "Back to Normal" was the cry, and by "normal" was meant a return to the serene world of Edward VII's reign. There was, however, and particularly among the returning soldiers, a sincere desire to improve social conditions. It should have been so simple. Britain had afforded £7,000,000 a day to defeat the Germans. Surely a fraction of that could be spared to fulfil Lloyd George's promise of "a land fit for heroes to live in".

At first it looked as though all the highest hopes would be fulfilled. Men poured back into Civvy Street to a booming economy. Trade union leaders, appealed to during the years of the fighting to support the country with all their power, though they had made concessions, had also not been slow to take advantage of industry's willingness to pay for their co-operation, and conditions and wages were vastly improved. Although the old cities, built by the nineteenth-century iron, wool and cotton masters, still stood, practically unchanged, at least the working man himself was better off and for the first time he had money in his pocket to buy a little of the comfort he had so markedly lacked before the war.

The General Election of 1918 was a shabby affair which did much to discredit Britain and the democratic system in the eyes of many nations. Lloyd George, the fiery Welsh lawyer from Criccieth, who had overturned Governments with his rhetoric and climbed to the premiership on the wreckage, was determined to get himself returned. He had never been a man of great scruples and now he issued official letters of approval to those candidates who promised, if elected, to support him. The Coupon Election, as it became known, returned him to power at the head of a Coalition Government after a period of mob oratory, in which the Liberal leader and his followers gave full assent to the wild cries of "Hang the Kaiser" and "Make Germany Pay". With him to Westminster went a wealthy body of men who in no sense represented the aspirations of postwar England. As Keynes said of them, "They are a lot of hard-faced men, who look as if they have done very well out of the war." It was these men who were called upon to deal with the first, hardly recognisable, signs of slump.

*   *   *

Prices and wages were almost treble those of 1914 and, for a while, industry thrived on the backlog left by the war. Nothing but armaments had been produced for four years and now the whole world was trying to catch up on the things it had so long done without.

In the spring of 1919, the retail price index – that measure of the change in the prices charged to the ultimate customer – stood at exactly double the figure at which it had stood when the war broke out in 1914. The rise in the cost of living was tremendous, but Britain was still –

formally at any rate, though it was growing more and more difficult as the problems mounted — on the gold standard.*

Prices were still rising, however, and if the British adherence to gold was to be more than a formality there would have to be very severe restrictions of credit: the bank rate would have to be raised, for instance, so as to make borrowing more difficult, hire purchase and overdrafts would have to be curtailed and investments inhibited. As in 1966, the price of strengthening the economy appeared to be a policy of retrenchment rather than expansion.

To start peace with a trade depression, however, seemed an appalling prospect. Accordingly, in March 1919, Britain announced the formal abandonment of the gold standard.

This policy gave the Government a little more elbow room to solve its internal financial problems, the most pressing of which was the need to find the means to meet current expenditure. Though a country, like an individual, can run on a deficit, public opinion at that time, both in Britain and abroad, demanded a balanced budget. This was one of the problems. The other was the need to do something about the load of debt left by the war, particularly abroad.

---

* A monetary system in which the standard unit is a fixed weight of gold. While gold coins no longer circulate in any major country, gold continues to serve as an international means of settlement between major banks. One of the advantages of the gold standard was that it limited the power of Governments to cause price inflation by excessive use of paper money. One of its disadvantages was that it made it difficult for a single country to isolate its economy from depression or inflation in the rest of the world. Hence it became normal for a country to break away from or 'abandon' the gold standard when it found itself in difficulties and needed to adjust its economy. It is argued nowadays that there is a substantial ground for using an independent monetary standard divorced from gold.

These debts were enormous. A great creditor country of the previous century, Britain now owed a vast sum to the United States for supplies bought during the war, and it was not of much comfort to her that she was owed almost the same amount by other nations, because the prospect of securing payment from countries which had been ravaged by the fighting was far from bright. Moreover, the sale of investments abroad to pay for arms had got rid of about half of her overseas credits, the yearly payment of interest on which had helped to bridge the gap between her imports and her exports.

Nevertheless, in the months immediately following the war, the need for goods and the eagerness of the men returning from the forces created a boom. Unfortunately, conditions had changed so vastly since 1914 that businessmen could only make a blind stab at the prices they should charge for their products. Demand for goods, moreover, was bound to be spasmodic since temporary needs, arising out of the artificial shortages created by the war, lay across the more normal patterns of buying. What also made pricing difficult was that the workers, encouraged by their union leaders, were already beginning to insist on more pay and shorter hours.

In the summer of 1920 the shortlived boom began to show signs of fading away. In April, the Bank Rate was raised to 7 per cent and borrowing became more difficult. To make matters worse, disagreements over wages led to stoppages in the important coal and cotton industries. Unemployment increased from August, and the year which had begun with hectic trade activity and a continued rise in prices, ended with trade deadlock, short time, unemployment, a very heavy fall in the price of wholesale commodities and a state of affairs where the general public was buying

as sparingly as possible because retail prices had not yet
reflected more than a fraction of the fall in wholesale
values".

There were other depressing factors.

Many firms had sunk more capital into their business
than the profit-making prospects warranted, and others had
acquired expensive equipment which could only make a
return if prices remained at a high level. Again, unscrupulous
war profiteers, seeing the red light earlier than most, were
busily unloading their factories and fleets upon a credulous
public still eager to make quick profits. Though prices were
outrageously inflated, everything that was put up for sale
was immediately snapped up and every share that was
offered found too many people anxious to buy.

The continuance of what was in fact war-profiteering
brought bitter comments about capitalist-conducted enterprise from Socialists like Ernest Bevin, general secretary of
the Transport and General Workers' Union, who saw firms
growing top-heavy and clearly heading for collapse.

One more thing, and by far the most serious, which led
to Britain's economic depression was her failure to recover
more than a part of her prewar export trade. Customers like
Germany were now too impoverished to buy, and the war
debts that existed between the two countries so bedevilled
trade relations that transactions became almost too com-
plicated to work. Moreover, as we shall see in the next
chapter, while British industry had been concentrating on
armaments, some of her previous customers had been
building up industries of their own to supply what Britain,
occupied with the war, could not supply — for example,
India, eager always for cotton for the ubiquitous dhoti but
denied supplies by manufacturers busily cashing in on
Government contracts, had started to manufacture her own.

What was more they had begun to protect their commerce from British competition by heavy import duties, while Britain still stood by the traditional idea of Free Trade.*

Britain's most serious rival was the United States, whose vast natural resources and population put her in a strong competitive position. Her very "newness" was an advantage. Partly because of the war, the older British industries had been allowed to become obsolete both in their technology and their economics, and the world conflict had smashed the trade pattern in which they had flourished. The Americans, with their readiness to experiment, their willingness to take risks with modern equipment, and their skill in salesmanship, pushed up productivity in the twenties by over 40 per cent compared with only 12 per cent in Britain.

With America as the greatest buying and selling nation in the world, the whole global economic structure began to depend on her. If she were forced by a diminishing demand at home to cut down her purchases abroad, her normal suppliers would also be unable to make their usual foreign purchases, and the whole cycle of world trade would therefore be affected. It was in this way that the 1929 slump in the United States became a world economic crisis.

---

* Free Trade is the economic doctrine that advocates equality of treatment for all goods for the purposes of taxation, whether produced at home or abroad. Protection or Tariffs—the application of duties on foreign goods, thus increasing their prices—is argued for those countries or those branches of industry in a country which cannot stand foreign competition. It was thought that Britain benefited from Free Trade. In the days when she commanded 50 per cent of the carrying trade of the world as an exporter, her free trade system made her ports valuable trading centres and kept London supreme in banking and finance.

Five / First Signs

ALTHOUGH Great Britain had emerged victorious from the Great War, she had suffered far more damage than at first appeared. She had started the first years of peace with an enthusiastic desire to get back to her prewar footing as a manufacturer and exporter, but she soon began to discover how far other nations not involved in the struggle had taken advantage of her total preoccupation with victory.

It was in the Lancashire cotton industry that the full effects of foreign competition were first felt. In 1914, three-quarters of their output was exported. By 1919, these goods were being produced in large quantities in Japan and India, and at a price, moreover — based on a lower standard of living and hence on lower wages — with which it was almost impossible for any Western nation to compete, In 1914, India had imported from England 3,000,000,000 yards of cotton goods. By 1937, our cotton exports to India had fallen to under 800,000,000. Though British goods remained unbeaten for quality, by 1935 Japan was exporting a far greater quantity, and the penniless millions of India were the last to complain if the cheap cotton they bought was shoddy.

For this situation the mill-owners of Lancashire themselves were largely to blame; they could not bring themselves to accept that the old days of prosperity were gone, and when they did recognise the need to introduce new and more economic methods and machinery it was too late. By this time, "the chaotic organisation of the industry", as its

critics pointed out, "contributed to its technical in-
feriority".

The story of coal was not much different. During the war
and immediately afterwards, when the industry had been
placed under Government control to co-ordinate the war
effort, coal exports from Britain were greater than ever and
the best seams – the higher and richer seams instead of the
more difficult deeper seams – had been recklessly exploited
and exhausted to get the quickest production. The destruc-
tion by the Germans of the French mines during the war and
the disorganisation of Germany herself following her
defeat enabled British coal, which cost 36s. 7d. a ton at the
pithead, to be sold abroad after the war at 115s., a not
insubstantial profit. Output in 1920 was 229,000,000 tons
and in 1923 rose almost to 1913's record figure of
287,000,000 tons.

But the days of cheaply won coal were over and the
industry was driven to the narrower and deeper seams. What
was more, in the first years of peace, as the Germans,
strangled by debts and regulations, began to realise they
had to work or die, the effects of German – and Polish –
competition began to be felt. Also those mines which had
previously produced high-quality coal for ships now
began to be hit by the change-over from coal to oil fuel in
marine engines. In 1914, nearly 100 per cent of the tonnage
registered at Lloyds was coal-fired. Twenty-one years later
this figure had dropped to just over 50 per cent.

The reluctance of mine-owners to introduce modern
methods of coal cutting also had its effect. While, by 1935,
nearly 80 per cent of coal produced in the U.S.A. was being
cut by machinery, in Great Britain the figure was still only
51 per cent.

In Great Britain mine-owners still relied too much on the

sinews of the men. Yet the miners' living conditions and the
danger and poverty of their lives were still like something
out of Dickens, and these were the cause of a long-standing
dispute between the miners and the owners which proved
a further handicap to production. The more far-sighted of
the miners' leaders demanded nationalisation as a means of

"DEAR ME!   HOW LATE 'THE ROCKET' IS THIS MORNING."

June 16, 1928

David Low, perhaps the finest of all political cartoonists, saw clearly how
out-of-date methods in British industry were leading to disaster.

modernising the pits, yet the owners, while too poor to
introduce modern equipment, still clung to their individual
methods and refused to combine.

In iron and steel, too, Britain was suffering from the
effects of production in the United States and from the
rapid recovery of the German Ruhr. By 1937, Germany had
increased her output to double that of Britain and the
United States to four times. Although Britain had added to

the capacity of her furnaces and adopted methods of mechanically charging them, a factor which, in the end, led to men being discharged, she was still losing her place in world steel production.

In shipping the war had had perhaps its greatest effect. Britain had suffered severely from the depredations of the submarine, and altogether had lost nearly 8,000,000 tons. Although this loss had been made good by 1921, foreign competition especially in Japan and the United States took advantage of Britain's preoccupation with replacing her own fleet to seize the overseas markets. During the war, the Allied powers had been forced to do all that they could to increase shipbuilding. The United States in particular had increased her tonnage by nearly 12,000,000 tons between 1914 and 1921, and Japan had doubled her merchant navy in the same period. In 1914, Britain had possessed 39 per cent of the world's tonnage, but she lost ground so rapidly that by 1937 her share had fallen to 26 per cent.

Thus, although the ravages of the war had been made good in the British merchant fleet, she had lost a great part, not only of her shipyard orders but also of her export trade. And while the volume of merchant shipping across the globe had grown considerably, the volume of international trade had begun to shrink, and tramp shipping freights on which much of Britain's prosperity had been based, also collapsed.

Finally, in agriculture a general rise in the cost of living and some exceedingly bad harvests had occurred just at a time when farmers were receiving less and less for their products. Although production costs and wages had mounted, farmers had not organised themselves at all and, in contrast to other countries where farmers had got to-gether to study foreign markets, they had no uniform policy.

The British shops were being flooded with cheap butter, eggs and bacon produced by Danish peasants who had accepted various forms of Government direction in marketing their produce.

In almost every field of industry, Britain was operating at a disadvantage.

Six / Exasperation

AT the beginning of the 1920s everything was pointing firmly to a trade recession. Prices reached their highest point in November 1920, and then rapidly tumbled. And as prices fell, unemployment rose by 75,000 a week. In November 1920, only 500,000 were out of work. By June, 1921, the total was over 2,000,000. There were more unemployed than for over a hundred years.

There had been slumps before, however, and only a few realised that this time the high unemployment was to be more than temporary. Everyone – of all parties – accepted it as nothing more than a phase which would rapidly disappear and looked forward to an early revival of trade.

Fortunately for those who were thrown out of work, the Lloyd George Government had fulfilled its promises of better conditions by recently introducing more generous unemployment benefits so that the hardships of the men out of work were never as bad as in the past. But Lloyd George, still trying to ride the crest of his wartime popularity was also forced to bow to the demand for unpopular measures in the curtailment of public spending. He appointed Sir Eric Geddes to the task of examining Civil Service expenditure.

Geddes, formerly general manager of the North-Eastern Railway, had been a deputy director of munitions during the war, and later – when Lloyd George began to doubt the ability as a military leader of Field-Marshal Sir Douglas Haig, the British Commander-in-Chief – had been appointed Director General of Military Railways. Entering Parliament, he had been Controller of the Navy, First Lord of the Admiralty and Minister of Transport, and he was now to become known as the wielder of the Geddes Axe, with which it was hoped he would save a sum of £200,000,000 a year by economies in expenditure on the Forces and the social services.

In effect, only about a quarter of this sum was saved but Geddes's name became a dirty word to officers who saw their service careers cut short through no fault of their own, and to those who believed that the new social services were the first step towards the New World they had looked forward to in the trenches. The distaste in the latter case was not unlike that provoked by the postwar Labour Government when, in 1951, in the face of opposition from Aneurin Bevan, then Minister of Labour, and the founder of the National Health Service, it decided, in view of the drain on Government funds, to make a small charge for various medical and dental services. Bevan resigned from the Government as a result.

Lloyd George's boast that "inhuman conditions and wretchedness" would be made to surrender like the German Fleet suddenly acquired a hollow ring. It was not perhaps surprising that the Coalition Government fell soon afterwards.

Lloyd George's genius was not suited to the drab mood of the first years of peace. His popularity, which had reached its zenith during the war, had declined rapidly and an unimportant but unsavoury scandal concerning the award of titles in the Honours List in return for money dragged his prestige even lower. Moreover, in spite of Winston Churchill's belief that the Liberals and Conservatives should combine to defeat their mutual enemy, Socialism, many Conservatives were anxious to throw off the shackles of

Lloyd George, crafty, clever, ambitious, a master of rhetoric, the man who destroyed governments and climbed to power over the ruins.

Lloyd George's Government and become independent once more. It was this which ended the Coalition.

The desire for peace, not only in Europe but in trade relations, was reflected in the ensuing election by the return of 344 Conservatives. Yet while the Liberals, pursuing their traditional behaviour pattern of disagreeing among themselves, were completely divided, the Labour Party's numbers in Parliament rose to 142, and Lloyd George was out of office for the first time in seventeen years. He never returned to it. Bonar Law's cynical remark about him "that the drummer boy was an asset in the hour of battle but that he and his drum were a nuisance in the hospital ward" proved to be only too true. By the time the next hour of battle arrived, he was too old to beat the drum again and there was a different and probably greater drummer boy.

Meanwhile Bonar Law, who took office in 1922 under the single-word programme of "Tranquillity", said "I do have at the back of my mind this feeling that in a condition so critical as ours the real cure must come from better trade and better industry". Unfortunately, while this statement was an unimpeachable one in itself, he quite failed to mention what methods were to be used and he headed a Cabinet which, as Winston Churchill said, was only the second eleven and was not eminently fitted to produce ideas.

*　　　*　　　*

Bonar Law took office knowing that he had only a short time to live. A year later he was compelled to resign, and before 1923 was out he had died. He has hardly left a mark on history, yet from 1914 onwards, his ability and self-effacing patriotism had been of the utmost value. As quiet and undramatic as Lloyd George had been fiery and full of wild Welsh rhetoric, he had made the coalitions of Lloyd George and Asquith, the first wartime premier, work smoothly. As Chancellor of the Exchequer he had raised the money for the war, and as Leader of the House of Commons in the postwar Coalition he had done much of the Prime Minister's work, leaving Lloyd George free to deal with the more spectacular business of peace.

His successor was Stanley Baldwin, who, born in 1867, had become an industrialist and only entered politics late in life. He had been Chancellor of the Exchequer in 1922, dealing chiefly with the vexed question of war debts, and, liking to picture himself as a sort of modern Walpole, the man who for twenty years had brought stability to England after the economic chaos of 1720, he saw his task as the restoration of prosperity and balance after the years of the war.

Behind his lazy exterior he was a shrewd politician, but the three Governments he led between 1923 and 1937 were to leave the nation in 1939 ill-prepared to deal with Hitler. Baldwin became, nevertheless, with his pipe and his pigs, the symbol of the trustworthy and country-loving Englishman and he put his stamp on the nation virtually from 1923 to 1937, throughout all the sad years of the depression.

Baldwin's first ministry lasted less than a year. He had inherited the policy of Tranquillity from Bonar Law, but he found this little remedy against growing unemployment. To overcome the depression, he proposed to abandon the traditional policy of Free Trade and substitute a policy of Tariffs.

In the General Election at the end of 1923 the country showed that, whatever else it wanted, it certainly did not want Protection. Although the Conservatives remained the largest party in the House, Baldwin resigned in 1924 to make way for the first government by the rapidly growing Labour Party. Although they could muster only 192 votes against the Conservatives' 257, they had been promised Liberal support in defence of Free Trade, and Ramsay MacDonald accepted office.

For the first time, the Government was in the hands of the working classes. In those days a working man capable of governing was an entirely new social type, and the members

Mister Baldwin

Stanley Baldwin, a shrewd politician but a man who left the country
ill-prepared to deal with Hitler in 1939, and came to represent the
Government's inability to deal with crises.

of the Cabinet were mostly men of humble birth. Both Ramsay MacDonald, a Scot, and his Chancellor of the Exchequer, Philip Snowden, the crippled Yorkshireman who was as much in command of the principles of finance as he was of the barbed ripostes of sarcasm, had known poverty in their early days and, like most of the rest of the Cabinet, had made their way upwards by sheer ability and desperately hard work. Then there were the trade unionists like Arthur Henderson, the Home Secretary, who had been a Tyneside ironfounder, and J. H. Thomas, the Colonial Secretary, who was the leader of the railwaymen, and was to become surprisingly popular with his good humour and dropped aitches. The King, George V, although unfamiliar with this new type of Minister, felt it was his duty to help them and went out of his way to try to understand them.

Born of the trade union and co-operative movements, the Labour Party comprised both the "hard-core" workers' leaders and intellectuals like MacDonald and Snowden who had aroused hatred throughout the country, even among trade unionists, by their unequivocal pacifism during the war. By now, however, the divisions had healed and it was felt that Labour was a twentieth-century party, without the clogging traditions of the Liberals or Conservatives and was therefore in a better position to solve what were essentially twentieth-century problems. There was, however, little suggestion of revolutionary Socialism. MacDonald himself, a handsome, theatrical-looking man with a musical voice but only vague and undefined ideas of social improvement, was contemptuously described by Lenin as "a middle-class reformer".

Because of their dependence on the Liberal Party for support, these men, from whom so much was expected, confined themselves to trying to prove two things — that a

Government of men from the working classes had the
ability to govern efficiently and that it knew better than the
Liberals and Conservatives how to run the country. In the
first it succeeded but in the second it failed — hopelessly.
MacDonald retained for himself the office of Foreign
Secretary, and showed undoubted qualities of statesmanship
that did much to improve relations between France and her
old enemy, Germany, but the extra work thrown on him
was to a certain extent responsible for the meagreness of the
Government's domestic legislation. In the autumn of 1924,
after the Labour Party had been less than a year in office,
the Liberals withdrew their support and the Conservatives
were returned to power with a clear majority of over 200.

Baldwin's second ministry ran its full course from 1924
to 1929 and while in its foreign policy it appeared to be
instituting a new era of international peace, at home it ran
full tilt into the drama of the nine-day General Strike.

*   *   *

The year 1926 brought to a head the bankruptcy of the
mining industry.

The anxieties in the coal industry lay at the heart of
Britain's industrial problems. There were at the time more
men in the industry who could not be profitably employed
in it than there were in any other British industry of the
day. For years unemployment had averaged over 16 per
cent, and although between 1924 and 1930 the manpower
employed fell by 200,000, the unemployment rate in the
industry remained 4 per cent higher than for the rest of the
country.

The trouble really went back to 1919 when, after the
miners had balloted in favour of a strike, a Royal Commission had been set up to investigate conditions.

Unfortunately, with three coal-owners, three industrialists, three miners and three economists sitting on it, the Sankey Commission was headed from the first only for complete deadlock. The proceedings included a great deal of baiting of coal-owners, and far less time was spent on the elucidation of facts than on the manufacture of Socialist propaganda.

In spite of the recommendations from the chairman, Sir John Sankey, who made a striking condemnation of the owners, that the principle of state ownership "must be accepted", nothing had been done. This, despite the fact that Lloyd George, the Prime Minister, had gone so far as to recommend early in 1917 a form of nationalisation, and had, in fact, put the mines temporarily under State control to help the war effort. The relations between owners and men had been bad for years, but the Commission only made them worse. Not even the slightest gesture of reconciliation had been made.

Nevertheless, in 1919, a seven-hour day had been introduced and by 1920 there had been considerable wage increases, partly subsidised by the Government in the hope of stimulating production. Unfortunately, production had not responded and when new wage demands had been presented, Lloyd George, as usual more concerned with his political position than anything else, had washed his hands of the mines. They were handed back to the owners, who were left to cope with falling demand, increasing competition, payments in coal of German reparations, and wage negotiations with a frustrated and exasperated labour force. A wage reduction had followed almost automatically.

Between 1922 and 1925 the industry had licked its wounds. There had been a small recovery, but by 1924 the industry was producing only the same amount of coal as before the war, but with 200,000 more men to do it.

Then in 1925 the plight of the mining industry dramatically worsened. In April of that year the country returned to the gold standard. The decision was taken, with Baldwin's full support, by Winston Churchill as Chancellor of the Exchequer, a post he had been offered to his own amazement as he knew nothing about finance. This had the effect of at once raising British prices by 10 per cent abroad.

*   *   *

As much as anyone else, this disastrous return to gold was the work of the Governor of the Bank of England, Montagu Norman, a man who, in spite of remaining in office for twenty-four years between 1920 and 1944 and stamping his personality across the period just as much as Baldwin, was singularly ill-fitted by nature for the job.

Artistic-looking with his pointed beard and sculptured profile, he seemed less a banker than an artist. But he was stubborn, narrow in his views, and according to Lord Francis-Williams, at that time financial editor of the *Daily Herald*, "charming and implacable, interested but beyond argument". Through his room at the bank there passed a constant stream of visitors from other banks, but rarely an industrialist and never a trade unionist.

He was a rigid advocate of paid debts, balanced budgets and a maintained gold standard even when it would have been much sounder policy to abandon it. He remained unmoved by industrial slumps, or the rise of unemployment which drove others to second thoughts. A man less inflexible might have accepted the need to pay regard to the internal as well as the external consequences of bank policy, but such moderation was not for Norman.

He had insisted on a settlement of Britain's war debt to

Montagu Norman, the "charming but implacable" Governor of the Bank of England, whose wrong-headed policies made the financial crisis deeper.

America, considering that anything else would harm London's international financial position, and had persuaded Baldwin, when he was at the Treasury, that this was a matter that touched closely on national honour.

Six months later, on July 7, 1923, the Bank Rate was raised from 3 to 4 per cent despite a Treasury warning that such a rise would have serious effects on employment. Keynes called it "one of the most misguided movements of that indicator that has ever occurred", because prices were falling and unemployment severe, and dearer money was bound to worsen the internal situation. But it was a necessary stage in Norman's campaign for a return to the gold standard, and two years later, in 1925, after a further rise in the bank rate to 5 per cent, he achieved success. Britain returned to the gold standard at prewar parity thereby pricing many of her exports such as coal out of the export market, provoking an attack on wages in every industry, and precipitating first the coal strike and then the only General Strike in England's history.

Norman was not alone, however, in his beliefs. Other economists — Keynes excepted — and politicians, who expressed their beliefs in the vague terms, "the pound must look the dollar in the face", took the same view. Yet, without the coal strike and the General Strike that the return to gold helped to precipitate, Britain might have had the opportunity to put through a thorough reconstruction of her basic industries at a time when there were still resources to spare for the purpose.

What was so extraordinary was that the experts couldn't see what ordinary people could. There is a cartoon by David Low, published in the *Evening Standard* in 1932, which showed Norman leading bankers in a round-the-mulberry-bush dance round a safe representing locked-up capital, all of them getting nowhere while the money was there to be used.

*   *   *

The origins of the strike of 1926 were similar to those of the interminable mining disputes of the years before.

"HERE WE GO ROUND THE MULBERRY BUSH"

October 24, 1932
Led by Montagu Norman, the experts continued throughout the crisis to do a ring-a-roses over the same old ground of retrenchment, while the money which could have set industry moving remained locked away.

The wage agreements of 1921 were terminated in 1924, and the new agreement, more favourable to the miners — because it was based on the one good year of 1923 — was out of date before it was signed. In the middle of 1925, hit by the rising prices following the return to gold, the coal-owners announced their intention to terminate this second agreement and, as a means of keeping the industry's head above water, proposed substantial wage reductions once more. The miners refused and, in view of the obviously unsound condition of the industry, the Government granted a year's subsidy to enable the owners to carry on without insisting on a reduction in wages. At the same time, however, they set up another commission under Herbert Samuel, a Liberal politician who had lost his seat in 1918. This committee produced recommendations far inferior to those of the Sankey Commission.

The Samuel Commission recommended, among other things, firstly that the subsidy, which had already cost the country £24,000,000, was unjustifiable, and secondly that there should be a voluntary reorganisation of the industry under private enterprise, something which, if it had been optimistic in 1919, was now quite laughable. It also suggested that means of improving the organisation should be agreed upon by the two sides—a fatuous proposal since they had been unable to agree about anything for years. The miners saw the answer in nationalisation. The owners, not the most efficient or enterprising of men—the Minister of Health, Neville Chamberlain, thought them "not a prepossessing crowd"—saw the answer only in wage reductions.

Their policy brought a prompt attack from Keynes. "On grounds of social justice," he wrote, "no case can be made out for reducing the wages of the miners. They are the victims of the economic juggernaut. They represent in the flesh the 'fundamental adjustments' engineered by the Treasury and the Bank of England to satisfy the impatience of the City fathers." The miners were, he said, being sacrificed to ensure the stability of the gold standard. Keynes was ignored.

Two months of negotiations brought no agreement. Finally the owners announced that from April 30th, 1926,

J. M Keynes

LOW

John Maynard Keynes, as often right as Montagu Norman was wrong, was ignored by the men in power until it was too late.

when the Government subsidy was due to end, they did not intend to employ men except at reduced rates. Not a single group of miners accepted. It was a virtual lock-out.

The sympathy of the working classes swung solidly behind the infuriated miners and a special T.U.C. conference on May 1st gave expression to this sympathy by their decision to call a general strike as a means of furthering the miners' cause.

Seven / The General Strike

THE General Strike began at midnight on May 3rd, 1926. The first to come out were the night compositors of the *Daily Mail* who had refused to set up a provocative leading article by the editor because they considered it was "insulting to the workers". On May 4th, the country woke up to find the railways closed and omnibuses and taxis off the street.

British industry and commerce were stopped dead in their tracks but, in addition, the nation was faced not only with a serious challenge to its economy but also to its whole political structure. A strike affecting the whole nation was absolutely without precedent. No one knew what would happen next, or how long food would hold out.

When it became clear that trade union leaders – chief among them A. J. Cook, of the Miners' Federation, who had made himself conspicuous by the violence of his language and his refusal to listen to argument either from conciliatory trade unionists or from politicians – were bent on an action which must result in a tremendous upheaval in the affairs of the country, the attitude of the Government hardened.

The strike, in fact, illustrated the class struggle in a most acute form. Those who worked with their hands were against the Government to a man, while most of those who worked with their brains or belonged to the non-working upper class were solidly against the strikers.

Baldwin could claim quite fairly that the strike was not

of his making. He had only inherited it. Moreover, for all his faults — and he has been credited with a great many more than he actually had — Baldwin realised the danger not only to his party but also to the country of stirring up passions when nerves were already raw with the protracted negotiations and frustrations. At first, while one section of the Cabinet, with Churchill as its most prominent member, favoured drastic action against the trade unionists, Baldwin contrived to divert their energies to less dangerous paths and appeared even to be more sympathetic to the cause of industrial labour than his colleagues thought he ought. He was not alone in his desire for peace, however, because most of the leaders of the T.U.C., responsible, cautious men like himself, were anxious to extricate themselves from an impossible situation with such safeguards for the miners and dignity for themselves as was possible. They were ready to do anything to reach a compromise which would allow them to call off the strike, and a formula was actually agreed upon which, though it was vague, held hope of a settlement even up to the last moment.

That hope was destroyed by the telephone call to Downing Street which gave the news of the strike at the Daily Mail office. This unofficial and unpremeditated action not only angered the Cabinet but destroyed Baldwin's last power to resist them.

The T.U.C. negotiators were summoned to Downing Street where they were met by Baldwin's secretary who handed them a note saying that "overt acts had already taken place, including gross interference with the freedom of the Press". The note made clear that the Government was not to be intimidated and that the strike instructions must be withdrawn before it could agree to continue negotiations. The T.U.C. leaders were baffled but, discovering what had happened, they drafted a conciliatory reply and two of them returned with it to Downing Street.

By this time, however, Baldwin, exhausted by the arguments that had gone on for days with members of the Cabinet and the trade union leaders, had gone to bed early, leaving orders that he was not to be disturbed. The T.U.C. delegates understandably concluded that they had been given the brush-off and that the Government was determined on a show-down.

Even so, they did not abandon their efforts and Ernest Bevin drafted and took to the Ministry of Labour a memorandum designed to offer a way out. By this time, however, Baldwin had made up his mind, and the strike that nobody wanted began.

Tuesday, May 4th, was the worst day. Transport throughout the country was almost entirely suspended, and those who were still working — who belonged to no union or were bound by apprenticeships or articles — had to make their way to factory or office as best they could. Men, women and girls packed the backs of horse-drawn drays and lorries and those with cars crammed them with passengers.

Volunteers, many of them university undergraduates prompted less by their politics than by their relish for a lark, rushed to drive trains and buses with enthusiasm — even if not always with the required amount of skill. There is an apocryphal story that one of them drove an express into Waterloo station twenty minutes ahead of time, despite the burden of two sets of level-crossing gates hanging from the front buffers. True or not, it typified the spirit of the days.

There were no newspapers, but Churchill himself, t combat the absence of news, made himself respons producing a Government news-sheet called *The British Gazette*, which the T.U.C. countered by producing *The British Worker*. And the Government made full use of broadcasting, though as most homes — and particularly working-class homes — still had no radios, the news they received was usually second-hand and often garbled.

In those areas of the coalfields where slack was available, cooking fires — in 1926 gas and electricity were not yet universal — were kept burning (or smoking to be more exact) by enterprising spirits who anticipated the future by manufacturing briquettes from coal dust, sawdust, cement and water. Nor was there any shortage of food. As the threat of some sort of strike action had been hanging over the country since the previous autumn, plans for food distribution had been worked out in advance and proved most successful. Hyde Park was made the centre of milk distribution, and food convoys were organised under military protection from London docks, though as nobody had any intention of interfering with food supplies, this seemed to be more a display of power than anything else.

In spite of the seriousness of the situation, the General Strike passed off with surprisingly little bitterness and no real violence — and often with considerable good humour. A great impression was made at Plymouth, for example, by a football match between the strikers and the police.

As the days went by and the country, in spite of the strike, contrived to limp along, the strikers began to see that their attempts to force the Government's hand had failed. Their efforts had come thirty years too late. In the days of horse-drawn traffic, a simultaneous strike of railway and transport workers might have been effective, but by 1926 there were other alternatives, and the Government had at its disposal a great fleet of lorries and cars in private hands and scores of amateur drivers willing to help. Realising that there was nothing to be gained by staying out any longer, some of the men started to return to work.

The more moderate and perceptive men among the leaders of the strike also lost their enthusiasm once it became clear that the struggle was not between themselves and the industrialists but between themselves and the Government. On May 12th, the T.U.C. finally admitted defeat and the strike came to an end.

The miners, their bitterness increased, stayed out, however, for several more months, but even among them the bite of hunger in their families was being felt. Men began to drift back to work, though such blacklegs were hated figures who had to be escorted home through jeering crowds of their mates by squads of police. It was towards these men that the only real violence was shown.

* * *

As The Times said, it was ridiculous to suggest that any considerable number of men were "animated by revolutionary motives", but no Government could stand idly by and regard the matter as an enlarged industrial dispute. "The General Strike," said Baldwin, "is a challenge to Parliament and is the road to anarchy and ruin." If the strikers had won, the Government would have found itself accepting arrangements it had already refused to make and which, indeed, it opposed; and the Government had been elected by the whole of the country, not merely by a small portion of its workers. The strike, in fact, raised the most serious constitutional issues. The question changed from "Who was right?" to "Were the unions to follow the Government, or was the Government to follow the unions?"

The whole affair did no one much credit. Lord Birkenhead,

a member of Baldwin's Cabinet, claimed that "it would be possible to say without exaggeration that the miners' leaders were the stupidest men in England – if we had not had frequent occasion to meet the owners."

Baldwin, however, enhanced his reputation with the firmness and sympathy with which he had acted to end the strike. He appeared to the country as the man who had stood four-square between the people and revolution.

Among the trade unionists, perhaps the only man to emerge with any increased stature was Ernest Bevin; in 1940 he was to become Minister of Labour under Churchill, with the difficult task of mobilising the manpower of the country by industrial conscription without exciting the hostile criticism of the Labour left-wingers. After the Second World War he became a formidable Foreign Secretary.

The General Strike not only brought little credit to anyone; it also achieved virtually nothing. Though it did not cause the depression, it certainly added to the difficulties that brought about its climax.

Days elapsed after the call-off before a general resumption of work took place, and the trade unionists were then shocked to discover that jobs existing before the strike had suddenly disappeared and 750,000 had been added to the unemployed. Before long, moreover, the miners found themselves in a worse position than when they had started. New agreements were concluded by the end of the year: hours were increased and wages reduced. Their persistence in fighting a lost battle had been calamitous for them, as well as for the whole trade union movement.

Mining itself received a critical blow because, in the seven months the miners' strike lasted, a powerful stimulus was given to the trend, already in progress, to substitute oil and electricity for coal; foreign customers explored the possibility of alternative supplies and came to the conclusion that some of them were cheaper and less liable to interruption through labour disputes. But if it did nothing else, the strike at least killed the illusion that, in the twenties, close on $1\frac{1}{4}$ million men could still get a decent living in the coal industry.

February 5, 1929

In spite of coal strikes which ought to have been a warning, the mine-owners' encouraged by official policies of retrenchment, did nothing to modernise the industry, preferring to wait, Micawber-like, 'for something to turn up'.

The loss to other industries cannot be assessed by any definite figure, but it was enormous and came at a very inopportune moment. France, at the time, was going through a monetary crisis, and the rapid depreciation of the franc more than ever disturbed the balance between the gold standard pound and other currencies; to maintain British exports, in which coal had played a large part, was especially desirable in these months. The progressive diminution of exports in the subsequent years was an important factor in the development of an adverse balance of trade.

On the other hand, though the miners gained nothing for themselves, their stand against lower wages acted as a warning to other industries, which were in consequence less willing to cut their own workers' wages. As a result, the purchasing power of the working classes was kept from disappearing entirely, as it was to do in America. There was always a shadow of production for home consumption during the dark years ahead when exports sank out of sight.

Eight / Over the Precipice

WHEN the General Strike ended, Baldwin's prestige in the country had reached its greatest height. He was regarded as the saviour of the nation and even in the bitter hard core of the defeated trade unionists there was far more respect for him and far less dislike than for any other Conservative minister.

Within a year his Government had passed the notorious Trades Disputes and Trade Unions Act.

This (1) declared that general strikes and certain kinds of sympathetic strikes were unlawful, (2) narrowed the right of picketing by, among other things, imposing new penalties for intimidation, (3) substituted "contracting-in" by which a would-be contributor to a trade union political fund had to sign a form declaring his wish to contribute, for "contracting-out", by which he declared his wish *not* to contribute, a very different thing and much harder to do, (4) forbade trade unions of Civil Servants to associate with the Labour Party or the T.U.C., (5) forbade local authorities to give preference in employment. By these and other means the law was stiffened against the unions. The result of the Act was a serious loss of union members and, in consequence a great weakening of the workers' bargaining power, so that conditions in industry worsened.

According to Lord Reading, the great Liberal judge and administrator and a former Viceroy of India, this punitive Act "offered no single ray of light for the British working man".

The initiative for the Trades Disputes Act of 1927 did not

come from Baldwin. Indeed, it was a measure which cut across all his efforts to project the Conservatives as a one-nation party. He would much have preferred to have trusted to the unions' own good sense, for which he had a considerable respect, to avoid a repetition of the General Strike.

Nevertheless, when it was presented to Parliament, he put his authority behind it and somehow, from this point on, Baldwin seemed to lose his grip on affairs and the Government fell more and more into what J. A. Spender called a "rest-and-be-thankful mood".

Ministers began to express the opinion that the Government had done all it could and that conditions were normal again, and that for any further improvement in the depressed trades, industry must look to itself. They attributed what depression there was largely to the General Strike and the coal strike, and, by inference, therefore, to Labour. Although unemployment remained steady at over 1,000,000, they performed a statistical sleight-of-hand to show that it was really less, since it included boys and women and a great deal of seasonal labour for which previously no provision had been made. If all was not well, they claimed, it was as well as could be expected.

And while the Government sat back, apparently satisfied with its achievements at home, Montagu Norman, still building on theories that belonged to a pre-1914 age, was engaged after April 1925, in a constant struggle to maintain sterling on gold "against . . . strains he could not prevent". According to Francis-Williams, his sole major contribution to the solving of Britain's industrial ills was to seek to promote "rationalisation" – the compulsory merging of firms into larger units and the closing down of "redundant" plants, without regard for the effect on the workers in them.

This policy reached its climax in the virtual murder of the shipbuilding town of Jarrow (see Chapter 14).

By 1929, as in 1964, the Conservatives appeared to have lost their sense of unity and purpose, so there was little

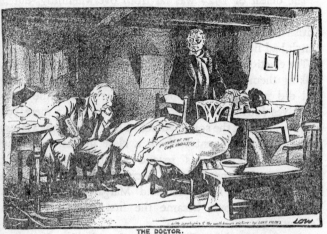

THE DOCTOR.

November 5, 1928

Using a well-known contemporary painting, Low represents Baldwin as the doctor to the sick coal industry. As Low wrote subsequently: "The sick industry is perishing miserably on its makeshift bed; the doctor sits petrified with sympathy, awaiting anxiously the result of his treatment— 'one tablet to be taken in a tablespoon of tears every session'."

surprise when they lost the Election, too. They had chosen the unfortunate slogan of "Safety First", and though this was actually meant to be a warning against the reckless legislation advocated by the left wing of the Labour Party, it was an unhappy choice of words with industry in the doldrums and trade falling, and men suffering the frustration of unemployment. It recoiled on their heads like the famous "Never Had it So Good" slogan of Harold Macmillan in 1959 (though the recoil in the latter case was to come five years later). A *status quo* was hardly the thing to offer to a demoralised working population and to industries which badly needed some impetus from the Government.

The defeat of 1929 was far from overwhelming, but it was sufficient to put in power at the most critical years of British industrial and commercial history a Labour Party which had little experience of governing.

The election had increased Labour seats from 160 to 287, making them the largest party in the House, though they still did not possess an absolute majority over the Conservatives (261) and the Liberals (now sunk to a mere 59) together. Against the sound advice of Bevin, who was against forming a government without a clear majority, Ramsay MacDonald formed his second administration. Arthur Henderson became Foreign Secretary, Philip Snowden returned to the Exchequer and Margaret Bondfield, as Minister of Labour, became the first woman to reach Cabinet rank.

Almost at once they found themselves faced with a crisis of a proportion that had hitherto not been known.

*   *   *

With things as they were, it was hard for anyone to believe in the last years of the 1920s that they were living through the upswing of a trade cycle. It was true there had been a small boom in 1928, but the unemployment situation was very little better in 1927, when there were 1,050,117 out of work, and 1928 (1,295,234) than it had been before 1926 (1,336,155 in 1925); the balance of payments — the difference between exports and imports — was more favourable, but only just; the country's share of the world's trade had fallen quite considerably (for example, British trade to the United States had fallen by 69,000,000 dollars' worth), and prices were still falling gradually, as they had done almost without interruption since 1922.

MOUNTS FOR THE POLITICAL DERBY.

June 4, 1929

The 1929 election (which took place in Derby week) brought little satisfaction to anyone. The Conservatives were out of office, though holding the largest number of seats. Labour governed, but only with the help of the Liberals under Lloyd George, the great war leader, who was thereafter reduced to taking a back seat. (J. H. Thomas at the horse's head, and Ramsay MacDonald 'up'.)

In the United States, however, an upswing which was also coming to an end, was equally not recognised because it was firmly believed there that the good times that the country was enjoying were likely to last for ever. From 1923 to 1929 the country had experienced "an era of prosperity approaching that of wartime" and its continuation was confidently forecast. "Our situation is fortunate," reported an expert economic committee, "our momentum is remarkable." Prices were surprisingly stable and therefore, it was argued, there could be no upswing with its inherent weakness leading to collapse.

For centuries trade figures had shown a cycle of booms and depressions and it was always felt that the higher the peak of the booms the deeper the depression that would follow. Small booms and shallow depressions were what most economists hoped for.

Unfortunately, the economic world of the 1920s was inherently unstable, and when the collapse began, it began in the United States.

For years in America the market had been saturated by consumer products, such as motor-cars and electrical appliances, and there had been a boom in building. At the same time, the country's financial policy of price stabilisation, while it kept the cost of living steady, not only concealed inflationary pressures and effects but also to some extent actually engendered them, because while productivity in industry had been increasing, the benefit of this increase had not been passed on to the public in lower prices or to workers in higher wages. Nothing had been done, therefore, to help sustain the purchasing power needed to take up the goods produced, and the successful businesses became more and more self-financing, which meant that they were less and less susceptible to control by the monetary authorities.

By 1929 the industrial boom was clearly over but a stock exchange boom continued. Deluded by propaganda which suggested that prosperity was permanent, thousands of unwise investors, loaded with high profits and infected by the boom psychology, maintained an orgy of crazy speculation in overvalued stocks. Unfortunately, the American banking structure was unsound and American enterprise in the twenties had opened its arms to grafters, swindlers, impostors and frauds. Everything was pointing to disaster.

In the autumn the crash came, triggered off, according to the New York Times, by the failure in August of Clarence Hatry's London banking house. Hatry had been arrested and subsequently convicted for a gigantic forgery of stock

THE MORNING AFTER.

October 31, 1929
Low's brilliant comment on the Wall Street crash. The great American spending and investment spree of the Twenties has ended in chaos and an appalling financial hangover.

certificates, and this started a wave of British selling in London and New York. This in turn set off a scare among American buyers.

And so, at last, on October 29th, 1929, according to one observer, "the gigantic edifice of prices began to break under its own weight. Down, down, down. The roar of voices . . . from the floor of the Exchange had become a roar of panic and huge blocks of stock were suddenly flung on the market for whatever they could bring." Brokers everywhere were fighting to sell; nobody thought of buying. And when the closing gong brought the day's idiocy to an end the gigantic record of 16,410,030 share transactions — as against 6,750,000 on a very buoyant day — had been set, and the average prices of fifty leading stocks, as compiled by the New York Times, had fallen nearly 40 points, when a drop of between 5 and 10 would normally have had banks worrying.

According to Spender, the American crash was "no gradual declension from prosperity, giving time for adjustment, but a sudden fall down a precipice almost in a night, with seismic results in all countries . . . depending on international trade". It rocked United States economy and shattered world trade relations for a decade.

In one month stock exchange values declined 40 per cent on the New York Exchange and speculators were at their wits' end to obtain credit to carry their losses. Agricultural values fell rapidly, dragging after them the world price for the principal products.

The depression proper had started.

*   *   *

In New York and Chicago, self-made men with vast new businesses and investors with old businesses who had placed their money unwisely, suddenly finding they could not face a future of poverty, took their lives by throwing themselves from the windows of their skyscraper offices. In Europe the financiers were watching the effects with increasing anxiety. The American economy was collapsing and world economy was leaning too heavily on it.

The end of the American boom would not have mattered so much if the rest of the world had been in a healthy economic condition. But it was not and the shock could not be absorbed. The world economy suffered from two great weaknesses, both results of the war, one general and the other largely manufactured by America, France and Germany combined. The collapse of America, at that time accepted as the most powerful economic unit in the world, exposed these weaknesses and turned them into crippling deficiencies.

The first great weakness, paradoxically, was that the world was cursed with plenty. The demand from Europe during the war had by 1929, with improved techniques of production, resulted in more foodstuffs and raw materials being produced than could be absorbed, and this had created a pressure on prices everywhere. When agriculturalists tried to maintain their incomes by increased production, prices were driven down still further. Unsold and accumulated stocks had been dumped on already demoralised markets at give-away figures and, when Russia suddenly began to emerge as a great wheat exporter at this time, prices sank out of sight.

The second great weakness was the structure of international indebtedness. Britain, the great prewar lender, was impoverished and her foreign lending in the twenties was smaller in volume and mostly for a shorter term than before the war. France had for years been affected by a flight of capital which had led to the holding abroad of large short-term balances – or "funk money", as it was called – but most important of all was the emergence of Germany, once a great industrial and commercial nation, as the world's greatest borrower, and America as the world's greatest lender.

The war had not impoverished Germany so much as people had at first imagined and the inflationary period of 1922–3 had forced her to undertake the renovation of her industrial equipment to help her survive. But she was still

E

hard pressed by reparations, especially as the general insistence that they be paid was being strengthened by American demands to countries like Britain and France that their war debts to America should also be paid. It was a vicious circle. To pay France, Germany borrowed from America.

With this great indebtedness, the world was treated to the spectacle of an annual flow of funds from poor countries to richer ones, an arrangement that would continue to work only so long as the richer ones remained willing to lend the money back again. Towards the end of 1928, however, American willingness to lend overseas suddenly fell away as American investors became preoccupied with the stock exchange boom. Europe at once felt the draught. It was only the loans from the United States that had saved the false façade of Reparations and international debts from collapsing. These, aided by loans from Great Britain, had enabled the European debtors to pay their debts with money provided by their creditors, and Great Britain alone was unable to fill the gap. American exports of capital which had amounted to 1,130,000,000 dollars in 1928, fell to zero in the next two years.

As a result debtors all over the world strove to cut their imports and increase their exports. Inevitably there was a further fall in prices. Then the American boom came to an end and the shock was felt across the world.

*   *   *

To begin with, Great Britain was not greatly affected. The bank rate was raised from 5½ per cent to 6½ per cent and, when the New York Stock Exchange collapsed, gold actually flowed to London for safety and it was possible to reduce the bank rate again. But eventually Britain, like every other country in the world, began to react to the increasingly fast descent of prices. During 1930 the wholesale price index in Britain fell by 18 per cent and the cost-of-living index by 8 per cent. Purchasing power of raw material-producing countries was meanwhile enormously diminished and British exporters began to suffer, Britain's share of world trade falling by about 7 per cent between 1929 and 1930. Profits fell, new industrial issues on the London Stock Exchange dropped in volume by almost one-third, and as the industrialists tried to stabilise things by cutting their costs, the British unemployment rate rose from over 10 per cent to almost 16 per cent.

The Labour Government of 1931, like the Labour Government of 1964, found itself in a crisis not entirely of its own making and, facing appalling and unprecedented difficulties, soon began to wish it had never won the election.

"Socialism In Our Time" had become the worst financial crisis the world had ever known.

Nine / Desperation

IN its election manifesto, the Labour Party had rashly undertaken to conquer the unemployment problem. Now, with horror, they saw it rise rapidly from 1,120,000 when they took office to 1,500,000 at the beginning of 1930, to 1,660,000 by April and to the staggering figure of 2,500,000 by the end of the year.

The boasted schemes of public works – like those in 1966 – which they had promised during the election came to nothing.* They could only just manage to hold their own, let alone pay for new schemes, and in addition there was the added worry of the Unemployment Insurance Act of 1930.

This Act, which had been largely based on wilful optimism, marked the extreme limit of relaxation of the restrictions on the drawing of unemployment benefit. During the twenties, benefits had been extended to all insured persons whether or not they had paid into the fund sufficient contributions to make them eligible members of a solvent scheme. Naturally the fund ran into debt. But no Government, least of all the Labour Government, too many of whose supporters were out of work, was anxious to

* The Queen's speech at the opening of Parliament in 1966 optimistically promised a more efficient working of the ports, expansion of agriculture, a financing of the coal industry, the acquisition of land for the community, subsidies to local housing authorities, a correction of the injustices in the rates, a development of higher education with more teachers, improved social insurance, an improved medical service and modernisation of the law, all in addition to the steel nationalisation promised in 1964.

introduce restrictions which would turn half-a-million unemployed voters into legal paupers.

Therefore benefit *as a right* continued and, in the words of

CART BEFORE THE HORSE.

November 30, 1929

Although the Labour Government had promised to deal with unemployment, they were preoccupied with social reform. This was praiseworthy but unworkable so long as industry remained stagnant. Ramsay MacDonald exhorts. This time it is J. H. Thomas 'up'.

R. C. Davison, in his book, *British Unemployment Policy*, the British workers acquired the habit of regarding the local employment exchange as "a sort of bank where, subject to rules, they always had a balance, and this sense of rights entered into the very grain of British social life".

By 1930 the Insurance Fund was over £100,000,000 in debt, but the Act which the Government introduced in 1930 in a fit of half-baked optimism made it still easier to draw money and actually improved the rates. All restrictions had been removed and, while previously, to prevent spurious claims, a man seeking benefit had to prove that he was genuinely seeking work, even this safety clause had now disappeared and anyone, whether genuinely in the labour market or not, could claim benefit. All you had to show was that you had worked in an insured trade at some time and were now not working – *even if you had no need to work*. The claims multiplied. The Act was unrealistic and ill-considered, and put the Treasury under even greater strain.

But if the Government and the Exchequer were suffering from strain, it was as nothing compared with the strain on the men who were actually out of work, in spite of the weekly dole from the Labour Exchange.

There were soon to be almost three million of them, or one fifth of the total working population of the United Kingdom. In some towns where the effects of the recession were most sharply felt, whole works or coal mines or mills had shut down overnight under Norman's policy of "rationalisation", and thousands of men were flung on the labour market at one throw, with never the remotest hope of their being absorbed into other jobs. In the areas worst affected, many were on short time or in and out of work for months – even years – and never had a chance to save up enough money to move to other parts of the country where, in spite of the slump, trade was still functioning and even making money.

*   *   *

The unemployed man spent his first day out of work dressing himself carefully, to hide the fact that his pride was hurt. He was often a skilled man and had never expected to have to ask for charity. He exchanged jokes with his mates about how much he was hoping to enjoy the rest and the change, but the jokes soon stopped and he found nothing funny in enforced idleness as it continued from one week to another. In the end, he ceased to care. He no longer had his best suit and collar and tie – they had long since gone to the pawnshop – and eventually the squared shoulders drooped as weeks went by of slouching on street corners. Finally he even ceased to bother about shaving.

The more energetic took to prowling the suburbs in search of odd jobs, offering their labour at cut-price rates, the weaker took to begging, and angry men took to wearing the medals they had won during the war and stalking the centre of the town with placards on their chest – "I speak four languages, served for four years in the army, have four children to support – and I only want one job."

Any work that was done in the unemployed man's family was done by his wife, and sometimes by his children. The war had proved that women and girls could handle machines as efficiently as men and for smaller wages. Often the head of the family had the humiliation of realising that his young daughter was bringing home more than he was.

"It was the boredom that was the worst," one of them said. "Not having anything to do day after day, week after week, month after month."

The out-of-work scarcely had the money to buy entertainment, though this was the era of cheap cinemas; the talkies had just arrived and it was possible still to get a seat for threepence. If anything flourished at this time it was the cinema.

Luxury picture-houses were still going up in the thirties, and significantly the most popular films were not protest pictures about poverty like Steinbeck's *Grapes of Wrath*, but the glittering musicals of Fred Astaire and Ginger Rogers and the society comedies of William Powell and Myrna Loy – films which enabled an unemployed man to escape for a time into a world of make-believe. Moreover, the cinema was warm in winter and continuous performances, which had just been brought in, allowed him to sit the show round twice and doze if he wished.

There was also always the library, and the reading-rooms were filled in those days as never before, though less with scholars than with men on the dole. As it seemed to be more important to protect the unemployed man from temptation than to give him even the slightest fillip in his dreary existence, the racing sections of the newspapers were carefully removed or pasted over so that he was deprived even of the minor pleasure of browsing over the winners he couldn't afford to back. But he could still hunt carefully through the *Situations Vacant*: it helped to pass the time, though if a job was going it was all too often filled without the need of advertising.

In the badly-hit areas, it was everyone's ambition to see his son enter a haven of security by getting a job in the local treasurer's office, or the gas works, or to become a policeman, a bus conductor or even a dustman. Favouritism was rife, and every town councillor seemed to have a relation in one of the council's offices. Applicants would go through the normal process of applying and even the farce of a short list, but the result was usually a foregone conclusion. The author certainly knows that he got his first job through the intervention of a local alderman who was a friend of his father's. In the distressed areas of South Wales and South Yorkshire, at that time, it was normal for half a class of boys leaving school to have no job to go to.

The young men took to back-street boxing matches and it became an age of professional fighters. As one of them said, "There was nothing like poverty to make a man have a go." There were football matches on empty patches of ground – none of the players having much in the way of equipment, of course – and there was a great deal of petty gambling. It was the day of the illegal street-corner book-maker, because the betting laws still enabled the wealthy man to have an account while preventing the poor from having a flutter. And there were pitch-and-toss schools in the woods, which were vigilantly sought out by the police – not so much because they wanted to persecute the un-employed but because England was still suffering from a Victorian narrow-mindedness about what could corrupt the poor.

Not only had they nothing to do, they had nowhere to go. "You see that corner," said a young man in the Rhondda to an official of a charity fund. "When I'm on my own my time is spent between here and that corner."

Perhaps the older men stood the idleness better. Many of them cultivated allotments which was a way of adding to the family's diet. Allotments are now somewhat out of fashion, but in those days whole acres were given over to small shabby squares under the shadow of the smokeless chimneys, each with its little wooden hut at one end, where the un-employed man could at least get away from the kitchen or the street corner, and where he could still feel a modest pride at doing some work. They were often sad little places, but they helped to keep a man fit and gave him something to do; they mattered a lot to his morale.

In the coal-mining areas, the unemployed miner's traditional load of coal, which was part of his wages and which was delivered by horse and cart and dumped outside his door, had ceased with his employment. Lacking coal for the winter or the money to buy any, the miners had to improvise other sources of supply. Where there were drift mines – a form of shallow mining where, instead of a perpendicular shaft, the mine entered at an acute angle because the coal lay close to the surface – they arrived in droves with their sacks and bicycles. What had been thick woods were turned into waste lands, as the trees as well as the shallow coal were removed. There are areas in the middle of the South Yorkshire coalfields which have not recovered even now, and still look like the blasted heath from *Macbeth*. Where there were slagheaps, miners organised parties to pick over the waste for odd lumps of coal which had slipped through the sorting machines; one would see endless processions of them pushing their cycles home with their dirty sacks drooping across the crossbars. Since the pits were closed, nobody cared much, though there were still occasional cases of trespassing brought before the courts. Poaching, of course, was rife.

In the worst-hit areas – those dependent on coal, cotton and shipping – the sense of desperation affected all classes of society. The unemployed man's possessions went to the pawnshop or to the butcher's or the grocer's to raise a little food, or to the pub to raise the price of a drink. Small shop-keepers kept books in which 2s. 6d. debts were entered and found themselves running an exchange mart for family treasures. A shopkeeper would always have great difficulty in deciding when to give credit and, according to the author's father, "Although it was difficult to refuse the pleas of the unemployed, if he gave too much he was out of business."

Most of the working classes who still had money to spend were buying at the market or the Co-op where there was a chance of saving a few pennies for Christmas, and, as it was easier for girls to get jobs than men, "they had long since," according to one of them, "accepted the habit of going dutch when they went out together or even of paying for their boy-friends."

When mill premises were put up for sale, there were never any bidders. No one was prepared to risk money, certainly not in the hard-hit North. Businesses were offered for a song — and yet there were still no takers.

"It was the sheer desperation," one businessman, who in 1930 was in danger of having to end a long-established family business, told the author. "We were chasing for money the people we'd sold to, and the people who'd sold to us were chasing us. There was practically no cash and what little there was seemed to be rushing round in circles trying to keep up with itself. We were waiting on the next small cheque to keep the doors open."

Cities that had thrived on their grime actually began to grow clean and in South Yorkshire, over the long rows of chimneys along the valley of the Don, the skies were clearer than for generations. J. B. Priestley found the unemployed playing table tennis in one of the clubs and centres which had been started for them by sympathisers like Harold Macmillan, then M.P. for Stockton.

"By the time the North of England is an industrial ruin," Priestley said, "we shall be able to beat the whole world at table tennis."

Ten / Vicious Circle

THE depression had a terrible effect on the morale of the country. The people lost hope, and it looked as though the Government had lost hope too. And it seemed to go on for so long.

In the years after 1920 the number of unemployed never sank below 1,000,000. During the depression of 1929–31, the figure rose from 1,250,000 to 2,750,000. By January 1933, the peak period, there were just short of 3,000,000. In the next years there was a decline, but, in 1937, in spite of rearmament and increased prosperity, the numbers again began to increase until by 1939 it appeared that the figure was steady at about 1,500,000.

At the worst period, there were four men for every job in the most depressed industries — coal-mining, iron and steel, shipbuilding and textiles — and there was a permanent hard core of men who had had no form of employment for over a year.

After 1933, when times grew better, it was noticed that the number of those long out of work still did not decrease. On the contrary, while in 1929, this hard core had consisted of 5 per cent of the total unemployment figures, by 1937 it had risen to 27 per cent. Many of the men were becoming unemployable.

Unemployment had become a social problem. The effect of prolonged unemployment on the man who was out of work and upon his family had to be taken into account. It wasn't a matter of statistics only. Until a man lost his job he had no idea how much the pattern of his life was ordered by his work. Now that he spent the whole of his life between his home, the Labour Exchange and the corner where he normally passed his days, the hardest thing to bear was the purposelessness of his existence, the feeling of being unwanted. To have to rely on Government charity, to be permanently at the beck and call of officials, however helpful, removed from him the sense of being able to decide any course of action for himself. Street-corner betting was often the sole chance for the unemployed man to make any choice between two alternatives. Worry and strain led to apathy and domestic unhappiness, and all too often where his children might gain a shilling or two in blind-alley occupations, the unemployed man was dependent on them for his pocket-money.

The poverty that was suffered brought the need for rigid economies. There was always the distance to be walked to the cheapest shop, and families went to bed early to save burning the lights and got up late so they would need no breakfast. Always it was the wife who bore the burden. In spite of incredible courage, standards began to sink and it became a vicious circle as the lowering of standards created an ever-growing number of unemployables. Poverty was found to be a cause as well as a result of unemployment.

The deterioration in an unemployed man was shocking as the weeks passed. The very sight of hundreds of other men in the same demoralised condition hanging about the centre of the town where he lived did nothing to help. With half the town out of work, he still had to line up three times a week at the Labour Exchange and had to go through the wretched ceremony of telling the clerk that he was out of work. There were queues of desperate men at the slightest rumour of vacancies at a works. But there was little pity left by this time. The works officials, normal enough men with their fair share of compassion, were sick of the workless, and most factories kept a sign constantly outside their gates, "No Vacancies", staring at the unemployed man like a sentence of death. The workless were becoming a nuisance.

Even if a man were willing to move to the other end of the country to get a job, he hadn't the means. It was nothing for a desperate man to walk thirty miles to the next big town in the hope of finding something — even on a diet of bread without butter and tea without sugar.

As the Dominions had been as badly hit by the slump as Great Britain, it wasn't even possible to emigrate. Up to 1914, thousands of people every year had gone to Canada, New Zealand and Australia full of high hopes, but they were now in just as bad a condition as they had been at home, and the young people from these countries, also affected by the world slump and as desperate as the British were coming to Europe to look for jobs. In 1931 more people arrived in Britain than went out.

Yet there were industries that escaped the recession. Counting private cars and commercial vehicles together, the number produced by the motor industry rose from 237,000 in 1930 to 404,000 in 1935, and employment in this and the aircraft industry rose steadily from 1930 onwards. In the electrical industries, the employment figure also rose — from 192,000 to 248,000 between 1930 and 1935. In the building industry, there was even a boom, which lasted almost continuously from 1924 to 1939.

In the more prosperous areas, where a lot of industrial construction went on between 1932 and 1937, there was an equally strong demand for houses as the number of families increased and the demand for rising standards in dwelling-houses brought about slum clearance. Moreover, the rise of new industries, mainly in the Midlands and the South, together with the spread of homes and factories into the outskirts of the towns, made possible by petrol-driven transport, created a greater demand for house-room. As a result other trades benefited — furniture, paint, glass, carpets, window-frames, concrete, stone, tiles and lead pipes, as well as electricity, motor-cars, lorries and motor-buses.

The more energetic from the badly hit areas tried to reach these more prosperous towns, some of them walking the whole length of the country on a carefully planned diet that was bought with their last savings. Certain northern towns lost 10 per cent of their population in this way, and as they were always the most intelligent and enterprising members of the community, the loss to the North is still being felt. Not all of them were lucky, however: the South was only relatively better off — it had a lower unemployment rate but there was still no great demand for men.

One of the bitter ironies of those days was that the people who had money found that, with prices falling, they were actually better off, and the unemployed were treated to the bitter sight of one section of the public actually enjoying themselves while they remained on the verge of starvation. Income tax at the time was no more than five shillings in the pound, and with even a few pennies extra on the tax a sufficient sum could have been produced to have got rid of the worst of the hardships of the unemployed. It would, in fact, have enabled them to start buying again and the movement of money would so have stimulated the economy as to boost employment. (For all its faults, the planned obsolescence of the years since 1945 has had the effect of keeping money moving.)

But what was more, with the money raised, the country could have managed to have put in hand plans for improving the sadly-neglected roads, developing the electricity

and gas supplies — to have dealt, in fact, with many of the
deficiencies that the country still suffers from to this day.
The cash was there, if it had only been drawn on; and there
was, of course, no lack of labour.

IN DIFFERENT WORLDS

April 17, 1934
**Self-satisfaction at Westminster hid the fact that the country had the power
to extricate itself from the Depression. The capacity was there and the men
were there and, in spite of Neville Chamberlain's begging box, so was the money.**

But the earnest wrong-thinking Norman was still at the
Bank of England, guarding what he believed to be the city's
and the nation's interests, which he considered marched
together, insisting on balanced budgets and clinging to the
gold standard with a rigidness that was almost pathological.
It was this gospel that coloured all economic thinking at
this time. It was unthinkable that Britain should run at a
deficit or abandon the gold standard.

Giving evidence to the Committee set up to investigate

Finance and Industry, and conducted by Lord MacMillan in
1929–31, when it was suggested by Keynes that half the
value of the bank rate was that it could affect the internal
situation, Norman denied that it did so. With Ernest
Bevin's questions, he was even more brusque. He refused to
consider the possibility of different rates for foreign and
home borrowers and displayed a complacency which,
according to Francis-Williams, "would have been remarkable at any time and was truly extraordinary considering
the state of the national economy". His one cure seemed to
be "rationalisation", and when Lord MacMillan suggested
that this was not the heart of the problem and that they
were perhaps dealing with financial problems with an
instrument designed to deal with other and more normal
conditions, he refused to admit that the financial machine
could be at fault.

He did not agree with Bevin that consultations with
labour were necessary to avoid vast upheavals of unemployment because, he said, "it was none of the Bank's
business," and, "he was even less ready to consider opinions
other than his own" when it came to a discussion of the
gold standard. The ills of industry, he claimed, were not
due to the return to the gold standard which had increased
prices by 10 per cent, but due to "certain misfortunes of
one kind and another". He refused to acknowledge that the
return had disrupted industrial plans and thrown the whole
economy out of gear and he remained optimistic about the
international economic scene, in spite of the clouds that
everybody else could see.

It was a tragedy for Britain at this appalling crisis in her
fortunes that her politicians had so little vision of their
own and allowed themselves to be bound by these rigid
doctrines of economy. Only a few people of influence in the

F

country like Bevin and Keynes disagreed with the Norman line. It was Keynes's view that, with all the available resources and techniques, the Western world was 'capable of reducing the economic problem . . . to the position of secondary importance . . . where it belonged".

However, Norman's views prevailed and there was no one in power who showed any imaginative approach to the problem such as that which Roosevelt was shortly to show in America. There, after the Wall Street crash, there were 12–15 million unemployed and millions were perilously near starvation, and the resources of State and Local Governments and private charities were well-nigh exhausted. But in March 1933, Franklin D. Roosevelt was elected President and carried through his revolutionary New Deal against determined opposition. Consisting partly of measures for recovery and relief and partly of measures of reform, based on the economic thinking of Keynes, it reversed all previous attempts to end the depression by ordinary deflationary means. Roosevelt, with almost dictatorial powers over industry, set on foot a generous programme of public works to stimulate business and help employment, aims which were helped by the devaluation of the dollar, the granting of loans and the abandonment of the gold standard. Similar measures were put in operation by Hitler, when he came to power in Germany in 1933, aided by the President of the Reichsbank, Hjalmar Schacht, though Hitler's plans were directed towards rearmament.

In Great Britain, however, the economists continued to believe that high taxes and public works would only increase unemployment; and the politicians, Baldwin and MacDonald, were not willing to risk going against what they were told by their experts. The result was that the economy, instead of being wound up tighter by the introduction of fresh money, was being allowed to run down by its with-drawal.

* * *

The year 1931 was even worse than 1929 and 1930, as the greatest international financial crisis ever known came to its climax. Falling prices, including share prices, began to put an impossible strain on the banks. On the Continent

VIEW FROM A SKY-SCRAPER

When Roosevelt (holding the flag) became President of the United States, the economy was deeply depressed and many of the banks had gone broke.

many had to stop business. This produced a widespread loss of confidence in European finance, made a mockery of international banking and led one country after another, because they were unable to realise assets held abroad, to "freeze" in turn their own foreign indebtedness. Austria was the first victim. Then Germany.

Then it became London's turn. London had lent liberally

— perhaps too liberally — and inevitably Britain was a major victim of the freezing of assets in European countries. Nevertheless other countries, finding themselves in difficulties, still continued to come to London for funds. But all unknowingly, some weeks before the Budget, the Government had dug its own grave. In an attempt to parry a Conservative vote of censure, it had agreed to the setting up of a committee to advise the Chancellor of the Exchequer on how to reduce public expenditure. The Royal Commission on Unemployment Insurance had complained the previous October about the unsound position of the Fund. Now the new committee, under the chairmanship of Sir George May, former head of the Prudential Assurance Company, forecast a Government deficit of about £125,000,000 and recommended economies of £96,000,000 of which £80,000,000, it said, should be found by reductions in the social services, which included unemployment payments. The money had to be saved within the year or the country would be bankrupt.

The Government had not foreseen the effect which the publication of this report would have upon foreign opinion, but it was immediate and devastating. The American crash had shaken credit in Germany and Austria and all through Central Europe, but it had still been believed that London was safe and money had continued to flow there. But foreign countries now got it into their heads that the British position was also insecure. France tried hard to recover its foreign balances before it was too late and financial conditions continued to deteriorate rapidly in those countries bordering on Austria and Germany.

London began to lose gold at an alarming rate. From July 15th to the end of the month, the Bank of England's gold losses averaged nearly £2,500,000 a day, whereas during the worst months of 1929, during the American boom, gold had rarely been lost at a rate higher than £250,000 a day. The bank rate was raised again but the drain continued. On August 1st, the Bank of England announced that a credit of £50,000,000 had been arranged with the Bank of France and the Federal Reserve Bank of New York.

The May Committee's report was a document of rigid orthodoxy – as Professor A. J. Youngson says, "it could have been written by Gladstone" – but it was supported by a statement from the Treasury pointing out that, even if borrowing for current expenditure on the unemployment and other funds ceased, there would still be the staggering deficit on the current year of £75,000,000 and for the following year of £170,000,000. And foreign opinion was demanding a balancing of the budget, and so long as it remained unbalanced the drain on gold was likely to continue.*

In the end there were only three possible courses open to the Government – abandonment of the gold standard, which almost everyone felt would be a disaster; unified international action to stop the world-wide fall in prices (there was no hope of this); or policies of economy.

The remedies suggested by the May Committee were not the kind to be easily accepted by any Government, least of all a Socialist Government. For the first three weeks of August, MacDonald and his colleagues vainly endeavoured to agree on adequate economies, but their Labour supporters

* The situation had a striking parallel in 1966 when there was a similar serious loss of foreign confidence in Britain's economy and a consequent ruinous run on her reserves. Once again there was a demand that Britain should put her house in order – and the result was a wage freeze and crippling restrictions on credit and investment.

were not only obdurate in their attitude to the cutting of
unemployment expenditure, but were even of the opinion
that no economies were needed.

While the Cabinet argued, the gold drain continued. The
Treasury was negotiating for a further international loan to
protect the pound, but it soon became clear that there was
unlikely to be help from anywhere unless the Government
showed itself willing to help itself by accepting some of the
May Committee's unpalatable suggestions. To the Socialists,
however, these pills were finally found impossible to
swallow and on August 24th 1931, the Labour Government
came to an end.

Ramsay MacDonald had not resigned. On the strong plea
of the King, who, going against all modern practice, invited
him to remain as Prime Minister when his Government fell,
he had agreed with Baldwin and Herbert Samuel (now back
in Parliament and leading the Liberals in the illness of
Lloyd George) to form a Coalition Government of all
parties. Its purpose was quite simply to save the pound.
Baldwin accepted the position of Lord President of the
Council.

MacDonald was followed only by Snowden, J. H. Thomas
and nine other members of the Parliamentary Labour Party.
Almost all the rest, who refused to support the coalition,
elected Arthur Henderson their leader, with George Lansbury
following him in that position later the same year, and then
Clement Attlee.

The feeling in the Labour Party for years was that the
coalition was a plot organised by Baldwin, the bankers, and
MacDonald who, according to Iain MacLeod, had been for
some time "expressing his taste for some form of National
Government"; that the King exceeded his constitutional
powers; that the crisis wasn't even genuine; and that the

Labour Party, which was coping adequately, was betrayed. None of this was true.

Nevertheless, with hindsight, it might have been better if events had been allowed to take their natural course and the Conservatives had come to power with Baldwin as Prime Minister instead of serving under MacDonald. It would have avoided the catastrophic split in the Labour Party which wrecked its value as an opposition for years to come. With Baldwin as Prime Minister, there would have been power with responsibility, instead of power without it, and Baldwin could still, if he had wished, have included MacDonald and any non-Tories who were willing to serve in his Cabinet.

But the strange four-year condominium which followed presented to the country a Prime Minister who had few supporters from his own party behind him – he was known to one newspaper as "the titular Premier" – and who, indeed, had become hated by his own party, and a second-in-command who led the largest party in the House. It was a thoroughly unsatisfactory arrangement, and it was allowed to continue for far too long.

However, the crisis had seemed urgent and the King was eager to help his country. No one foresaw that the Labour Party would turn its back so firmly on MacDonald, and it was felt with good reason that, with unemployment as high as it was, a Labour Prime Minister would be able to unite the country more effectively for sacrifices than a Conservative.

As it happened, by means of orderly finance and a tariff which, though it bore hard on the special areas, did in fact stimulate internal trade, and helped by a house-building boom in 1934–5 and finally by rearmament, the National Government did extricate Great Britain from the worst of

the depression. But the tragedy of the thirties was that the
crisis with which Britain was finally faced was not economic
at all but political and military, a crisis of foreign policy and
naked aggression from Germany and Italy, which both
MacDonald and Baldwin were sadly ill-fitted by tem-
perament to solve.

Eleven / The Naval Mutiny

As soon as the Labour Government resigned and the National Government took office, world financiers reckoned that wild schemes of national expenditure had come to an end and that Britain was doing something to help herself. The drain of gold from London diminished at once.

The pound remained very weak, however — there was still a deficit of £23,275,971 and an unemployment figure of 2,762,219, but on August 28th, Norman obtained credits in Paris and New York amounting to £80,000,000,* and on September 10th, Snowden introduced a revised Budget which was designed to balance the national accounts and effect a saving of £70,000,000.

The international economic situation was still degenerating, however, and a new and unexpected pressure was to build up on sterling. To save funds, cuts were made in the pay of the Services and other Civil Servants. Immediately, to the surprise of everyone but the men involved, there was a short but spectacular demonstration of protest on board several ships of the Atlantic Fleet at Invergordon, the largest naval assembly in the world at the time, which became known as the Invergordon Mutiny and which was to have a further drastic effect on the hard-pressed British economic system.

*   *   *

* Compare this with the British debt to the International Monetary Fund at the end of 1964 which, according to the Annual Register, amounted to £991,000,000.

Conditions in the Navy had been sadly neglected during the First World War. Pay and allowances were so small that a man with three good conduct badges, representing thirteen years of faithful service, could have a daughter of sixteen earning more than he was. The situation was little better in 1931, with unfair discrepancies not only between ship and shore but also between the various grades of the sailors themselves.

The officers were equally angry. The Geddes Axe (see page 35) had uprooted more than 1,200 lieutenants and lieutenant-commanders from their chosen careers with only a small gratuity and an even smaller pension. There was a growing sense of insecurity, and both officers and men felt they had been betrayed, particularly as shortage of personnel had so reduced a man's time ashore that the old naval prayer about returning to enjoy the blessings of the land had become nothing but a mockery.

This was not the only cause of unrest. There was also the influence of Communism. During the Russian revolution of 1917 and the civil war that followed, certain ships of the Fleet had been into Russian ports. Still others had been infected by the strong Communist cells in German ports during the twenties.

Also, after several years of peace, many of the wartime crews had disbanded and new men, bitter because they had been forced by the absence of work ashore to join up, had found their way into the Fleet. They had none of the spirit of earlier recruits and, having previously been members of trade unions, they did not hesitate to air their grievances. And they included a number of professed Communist agitators who did not fail to take advantage of the feeling of frustration that had become so prevalent.

The decision to cut pay might still have passed off

without trouble in the Navy as it did in the other services, but both bad luck and bad judgement intervened.

The ships of the Atlantic Fleet that began to sail northwards from their home ports on September 7th, contained a number of agitators who were determined to make the maximum political capital out of the May Committee's report on economy. In view of the general unrest, it was essential that officers in command should have full knowledge of the proposed measures of economy. This was realised by the Admiralty, who arranged for a signal to be sent to commanders-in-chief all over the world, explaining the position and the sacrifices demanded.

This signal was received by every commander-in-chief except the Commander-in-Chief, Atlantic Fleet, though it reached H.M.S. Nelson, his flagship. Unfortunately Admiral Sir Michael Hodges was not on board, and when he returned from leave he was not shown the signal at once; and almost immediately he became seriously ill with pleurisy and was rushed to hospital.

The sailing of the Fleet was not cancelled, but the admiral's illness led to confusion, and Rear-Admiral Wilfred Tomkinson, who had taken over, sailed in command in a different ship, H.M.S. Hood, without having any inkling of the imminent pay cuts. Nelson was left behind with the Commander-in-Chief's staff and, of course, the all-important signal.

This was not the end of the confusion. A letter, issued by the Admiralty on September 10th explaining the reductions might have put things right but, due to various departmental muddles, it did not reach Rear-Admiral Tomkinson at Invergordon until four days later, September 14th, three days after details had already been released to the Press.

* * *

As soon as the ships were anchored in Cromarty Firth, boats went into Invergordon for the post and newspapers, and those senior officers who had heard of the impending pay cuts from the B.B.C., felt sure there would be an official explanation from the Admiralty in the mails. There was no word, however, but the explosive accounts of the proposed cuts in the Press were immediately seized on by the lower deck; the calls for self-sacrifice provoked only bitter laughter, that was made more hollow by the mis-leading way in which the cuts were set out — as reported by the less responsible papers, they seemed to affect only the lower ranks. The agitators claimed, not without justifica-tion, that the reductions in some cases would force men's wives to the point of starvation and even to prostitution, and coming unannounced as they did, they left the sailors with a feeling that their superiors at the Admiralty couldn't care less.

It seemed, in fact, that officers drawing £2,000 a year and upwards were to receive cuts of 10 per cent, and other officers from 10 per cent to 3 per cent, while an able seaman's pay was to be reduced from 4s. od. a day to 3s. od. a day, a figure of 25 per cent. This assumption was incorrect as it took no account of allowances, but, without the benefit of official explanations, the interpretation put upon the newspaper announcements was inevitable.

Other sections of the public affected by the cuts, such as the teachers, were already protesting loudly to the Govern-ment, and representatives of the Communist Party hurried north to take full advantage of the unrest in the Fleet.

Mass meetings were held by liberty men — men on pass — in shore canteens, but were investigated only after they had broken up, and it was reported to Rear-Admiral Tomkinson that the rowdyism was due only to a small majority of the sailors having had too much to drink. The truth was that plans had already been laid for collective strike action and the men had returned to their quarters to inform the rest of the crews and select leaders.

The Admiralty letter outlining the pay cuts, when it finally arrived, though it made nonsense of the more lurid newspaper reports, nevertheless contained several blunders, and its tone suggested that it had been drafted by people completely out of touch with the problems of the men. What was worse, it arrived too late when feeling in the ships had already hardened and when the men were in no mood to listen.

Early in the evening of September 14th, a large number of liberty men began to gather once more in the canteen ashore and there were inflammatory speeches from those sailors with Communist sympathies. The lieutenant in charge of the shore patrol tried to gain a hearing but he was roughly handled. An emergency patrol sent on his instructions found the canteen deserted. The men had wisely dispersed to a recreation ground not far away, and here the final decision to strike was taken.

On Tuesday, September 15th, the ships were to go to sea. In some ships, there were already unmistakable signs of disaffection, and men were disappearing from work on the flimsiest of excuses. When the time came for the anchor to be weighed on H.M.S. *Valiant*, the first ship to leave, her crew stood or sat on the cable so that it became impossible to weigh without inflicting injury on them. The captain reported to the admiral who had no option but to withdraw sailing orders.

Although shore leave was stopped the news of the trouble spread rapidly and journalists began to follow the professional agitators towards Invergordon in great numbers.

By dusk the whole length of the coast road along the shore of the firth was lined with cars.

*   *   *

It looked like deadlock. Two officers were hastily sent south to convince the Board of Admiralty in anything but diplomatic language of the need to investigate the grievances on the spot. Needless to say, their pleas produced no such result. Nevertheless, they did manage to convince the Admiralty of the danger of the situation. Somewhat unwisely under the circumstances, the Board insisted that the ships must sail south, but it promised an investigation and the alleviation of hardship; and it dropped a strong hint that further disobedience would be heavily punished, but that there would be an amnesty against all those who had transgressed up to that point.

By the 16th, it was all over. The men knew they had gone too far and that what the agitators had told them was only a strike was in fact a mutiny in the eyes of the Navy. The hints were enough. Largely due to the good sense of certain popular commanding officers and in spite of the continued efforts of the agitators aboard, the ships weighed anchor. By the 28th, a new Commander-in-Chief had been appointed and those men who were considered to have brought about the mutiny were either drafted out of the ships and dispersed or discharged from the Navy. At the Admiralty, there were the usual polite evasions and the selection of scapegoats, and the mutiny was considered over.

It had been only a localised affair which did not affect the rest of the Navy where the Admiralty letter had arrived on time, but for a while it had seemed that an unwise decision at Invergordon would produce a tragedy of enormous significance that could affect political decisions not only at home but throughout the British Empire. The description of events at Cromarty Firth in the Press, and the Admiralty admission that the Fleet — that most hallowed of service institutions, which to most people still seemed symbolic of the strength of Britain — had mutinied, caused a tremendous shock throughout the country and throughout the world.

The consequence was a further financial panic. Over £30,000,000 of gold was lost within three days, four times as much per day as during the disastrous days that had followed the May Committee's report and forty times as much as during the critical period of 1929. As a result, the credits of £80,000,000 negotiated by Norman in August were soon almost exhausted. To the desperate men in London, there seemed only one last resort and on September 21st the Bank of England was compelled to ask for authority to suspend the gold standard.

None of the things to which Norman had pinned his faith seemed safe. The magnificent edifice of international confidence and stability he believed in and for which the temporary distresses of industry were in his opinion but a small price to pay, was only a house of cards that had collapsed before the economic blizzard sweeping the world — only six years after he had built it and within three months of his evidence before the MacMillan Committee!

Thus, as a direct result of the activities of a few agitators in the Fleet, the much vaunted and hard-fought-for gold standard had vanished. Falling prices in a world ridden by unrealistic indebtedness had created a situation which required some financial centre of enormous strength. Judging by the economic results of the naval mutinies, London was not that centre, though, with the arrival of Roosevelt's New Deal and the advent of Hitler in 1933, it became once more the only market in which money could be deposited or from which it could be withdrawn with perfect freedom.

As it happened, though, the immediate consequences of the abandonment of gold were not serious. Although the public had been taught to believe it would be calamitous, the departure from gold actually gave a fillip to foreign trade without disturbing the purchasing power of the pound at home, while the dollar, sapped by the persistent weakness of the American economy, fell. The American financial situation continued to deteriorate because many countries had now decided it was safer to back their currency with gold instead of dollars and this put further pressure on the dollar. This further weakened confidence; and the hoarding of currency in America, because of the doubtful state of the banks, became widespread. Other countries like Greece and the Netherlands, however, also had their economies upset by the fall in the value of their sterling reserves. Scandinavian countries, who were also on the gold standard, and most of the countries of the Empire had followed Britain's example.

Britain's abandonment, however, brought to a head largely by the mutinies at Invergordon, had consequences of the utmost importance in the years that followed. As far as Britain herself was concerned, the direct results of the abandonment were almost wholly favourable; but according to Professor Youngson, the indirect and remote consequences, and particularly the setback to international economic co-operation in general and the resultant rise of nationalism, suspicion and hatred in Europe, were without doubt disastrous. Though the agitators had certainly never intended anything quite so far-reaching, the mutinies were to affect indirectly the whole economic system of the world.

Twelve / The Last Straw

THERE had originally been no intention of holding an immediate General Election, for although very few Labour M.P.s backed MacDonald, Conservatives and Liberals combined were a majority in the House. But in October 1931, Conservative pressure on Baldwin forced the issue and MacDonald was obliged to dissolve Parliament.

He asked for a "doctor's mandate" to restore the nation's economy, using any remedies, including tariffs, that were found to be necessary. The results of the election in November were an overwhelming victory for the "National" parties with 556 seats to 55. It was the 1918 election all over again, with Lloyd George this time on the losing side. These events divided the Liberals, most of whom stood by Free Trade, and created a rift in the Labour Party that remained for years. They never forgave MacDonald. Out of 289 Labour M.P.s in the previous Parliament only 46 survived, and all the big names had been rejected.

The National Government's two avowed policies had been to balance the budget and save the gold standard. It more or less managed the first, but had already come to grief on the second. Now, reluctantly it adopted a policy of Protection. Falling prices, the non-renewal of foreign loans, the freezing of assets and Britain's abandonment of the gold standard had put terrific pressure on all countries to export. But these exports were most unwelcome in other countries because they only served to intensify unemployment and drained away reserves of foreign currency. The protective measures that were adopted in Britain invited and produced

retaliatory measures and had the effect of increasing the
tariff wall round the Empire.

Denmark, the Argentine and Germany were the hardest
hit. Banks in Berlin were forced to close their doors and
such was the pressure there that Germany's desperate people
began to turn from the bankrupt policies of their leaders to
those of a megalomaniac orator, Adolf Hitler, who rose to
power in 1933.

*   *   *

Meanwhile the depression persisted. Although by 1932
the link with gold had been severed and a new scheme, the
Exchange Equalisation Account instituted by Neville
Chamberlain, who had become Chancellor of the Exchequer, was keeping a tight control on sterling, the unemployment figures had improved only slightly to
2,800,000 and were to grow worse again in 1933. And
while Keynes and other economists at home and abroad
were stressing that excessive saving in an industrial system
geared for mass production and demanding a high rate of
spending by the mass of the people would have damaging
effects, Chamberlain was busy urging the ordinary people of
Britain to save harder than ever. State planning of public
works to reduce unemployment had been recognised as
necessary in almost every other country in the world, but
Chamberlain remained convinced that it would be blas-
phemous to interfere with the free working of uncontrolled
private enterprise. Following on Norman's disastrous
policies it gave British industry no chance to recover its
strength.

*   *   *

The depression was now entering its worst phase and, for
those who had been out of work for a long time, in some

cases years, there were no longer any reserves of money or energy or hope to fall back upon.

In shipyards along the Tyne they had worked hard till the last moment, the whole area round the shipyard clamorous with the sound of the riveting and welding that so often made the older workers deaf. But as each ship had been launched and the sirens had hooted, the men had cheered with heavy hearts, knowing there were no further orders. As the yards fell silent, it was as though a great machine had been switched off. Where the shipbuilding was carried on right in the centre of a town, it was as though the heart itself had been torn out of the place.

Now that there was so much less trade, even the ships that had been built before were often idle, and along the Tyne, the Tees, the Mersey and other great rivers there were no longer enough berths for the redundant vessels. Many of them turned up, anchored in great strings, in the rural inlets of the West Country like Bideford and Fowey. Leo Walmsley paints a vivid picture of red rusting ships laid up unwanted in Cornwall, often with a man living with his wife aboard one of them as watchman for the whole lot.

Only fifty years earlier, Britain had built 80 per cent of the world's shipping, but her share now in the world's output was only one third, and the merchant fleet had shrunk to a fragment of its former size. Captains were forced to go to sea as mates and mates as bosuns, and many seafaring men left the sea never to return, so that towards the end of the thirties, when the threat of war demanded a new build-up, it was possible for almost anyone who could stand upright to get a job aboard a ship leaving England. In 1938 ships went to sea short of experienced men or with sick or crippled men among their crews.

*   *   *

Unemployment benefit had been 25s. od. a week for a man with a wife and child – up to 1930 when it was raised to 28s. od. – but the increase brought little joy (it would be worth about £3 10s. od. at present values) and between 1931 and 1934, under the National Government's economy plan, these payments were reduced by 10 per cent. Even then there were some families who managed, with energy and intelligent management, to keep their pride in a clean home. But there were many where the cuts came as the last straw and all pride vanished in squalor and misery.

One case, quoted in a report to the Pilgrim Trust, was "in a typical Liverpool family where there were two children . . . The family had nothing but bread and margarine and tea with condensed milk, for breakfast and dinner. 'But,' they said, 'we always try to give the children something hot for tea, and go to bed early so as not to feel hungry.'"

In another case of a young couple, interviewed at three in the afternoon in February with snow falling, "although the house was neat there was no fire and so far that day they had had nothing to eat, only cups of tea . . . they weren't starved though sometimes they had to go pretty short."

When a man had exhausted his benefit, which could take anything up to six months, he went on to the dole proper. The money he drew remained the same, but the humiliations which the Means Test imposed on him marked his life for ever.

One of the first acts of the National Government had been to set up this dual scheme of payments to the unemployed which differentiated between the insurance benefits drawn as a right and a secondary scheme which was operated on the basis of need – or the Means Test; simultaneously insurance benefit rates both in amount and duration were reduced. Moreover, to qualify at all the claimant now had to prove that he had paid thirty contributions in the previous two years. These restrictions disallowed over a million claimants at once. For these people there was now only the Means Test, and this meant the humiliation of the official inquiry into their private affairs, and the doubtful justice of helping those who had not bothered to save and compelling those who had saved for the rainy day to part with their savings in order to receive State assistance. Also, in many a proud workman, there was the stigma of having to apply to the Poor Law.

To this day the words "Means Test" are associated in what were the Depressed Areas with evil and inhumanity. The bitterness left by the cut in the dole was nothing compared with the loathing that was felt for the Means Test. Nevertheless, 200,000 people ceased at once to be applicants for assistance and a sum of £10,000,000 a year was saved. This and other small savings were perhaps the justification for the system.

"It was not that it saved money by cutting down the allowances of those poor people who were assisted," it was argued, "but that it was a way, perhaps the only way, of keeping off thousands of applications from people who, though not in need, took advantage of State 'doles' given as a right without the condition of making contributions."

The Means Test was so loathed, however, that some Town Councils flatly refused to administer it and the Government had to send out officials to act for them. A man could lose his benefit if he had bought his own home or had paid off part of it. He could be required to withdraw every last red cent of his savings and sell his furniture, curtains and anything that added a scrap of comfort to his life — and sometimes he was. There were even stories of allowances for babies being refused if the mother breast-fed the child.

Perhaps worst of all, however, was the provision that laid down that an unemployed man should first draw on what resources his family could provide before demanding assistance. A woman working part-time was expected to keep her husband. A daughter who was fortunate enough to have some trivial job as a typist would be expected to hand her wages in entirety to the household income, and the family's benefit would be cut according to what she earned. Men living with relations lost their benefit because it was expected that they should be kept by their family.

This issue of "family responsibility" roused the deepest resentment of the whole depression — resentment and shame and bitter anger, because without doubt it led to the breaking up of more than one tightly-knit family where a growing child, eager to make his way in the world, felt he could no longer accept responsibility for keeping his older relatives. Although they were designed to help, so many of the things the Government did seemed a direct blow to pride and dignity and this was the hardest thing of all to bear.

As the Means Test reduced payments to the unemployed, the pawnshops became jammed with goods which the pawnbroker did not even want and which, in most cases, could raise only a few shillings. After a while, pawnbrokers refused to accept any more furniture because it took up so much space; only clothes and bedding remained easily pawnable because, being virtually indispensable, they were the only things likely, sooner or later, to be redeemed.

You paid extra to have your best suit put on a hanger instead of having it placed folded on a shelf, and the family wardrobe would disappear when money began to get tight and reappear only when money became available again. Unlicensed moneylenders did great business by lending a shilling at a penny a week interest.

There was nothing left. "It was pathetic," said one veteran Sunderland politician, "to see women shivering in winter in their cotton frocks."

At Christmas, charitable collections were made to buy meat for the unemployed and soup kitchens in cold weather sold bowls of soup at a halfpenny a time. Sometimes, even, these soup kitchens were organised by the unemployed themselves, who begged scraps of meat from the butchers. The author's father arranged for fish to be bought cheaply in Grimsby and transported to Rotherham where it was sold in his garage to the unemployed who waited for hours for it.

Union organisers, knowing they could never achieve anything for their members, still went on trying if only to convince the unemployed that someone was taking an interest in them. But it was a period of misery and humiliation and of class hatred, and it did irreparable harm to the Conservatives, who made up the bulk of the National Government. Whole towns turned their backs on the Conservatives for ever, and Britain became once more two nations, with the dividing line drawn somewhere north of London.

To the hard-hit North, the Labour Party meant men of their own type who suffered with them. The Conservatives meant moneyed men from the South who could not hope to understand their difficulties. Even the well-meaning organisations in London that organised relief seemed to do it in a way that emphasised the difference between the Haves and the Have-Nots, and bitter cartoons were produced of unthinking white-tied men and evening-gowned women eating colossal meals with champagne while launching their appeals for charity. To this day, Northerners still regard the South — because it never experienced the worst of the depression — with suspicion and resentment.

They remember only too well that young men joined the army to get a job, and that when war came in 1939 many of the Territorials who disappeared to France to die at Dunkirk had first joined only to get a decent pair of boots.

ELECTIONEERING IN DARKEST BRITAIN.

October 23, 1935

To the slump-hit north, the Conservatives who chiefly constituted the National Government, were well-fed blimps from the South with no understanding of what the North had to endure.

They still find it hard to forget the poverty and the hunger, the malnutrition and the tuberculosis that resulted. The Conservatives, they felt, didn't care.

In actual fact, the depression was not the fault of any particular party, any more than it was the fault of a particular section of the country. The parties merely inherited each other's mistakes and made them worse by more of their own.

Thirteen / The Town That was Murdered

By 1933, the situation had begun slowly to improve – not only in Britain but also abroad.

In England, business had been at its worst in 1931 and the outlook in 1932 was still sombre. Nevertheless, for the businessman and the investor things were just a little brighter. As a result of their economy measures, the Government had accumulated sufficient gold by February 1932, to repay the credits given in 1931 to defend the pound, and the bank rate was accordingly lowered. By this and other means, people gradually began to be convinced by 1933 that the economy was being soundly managed, certainly as soundly as any other country's, and that the situation was unlikely to deteriorate further.

Meanwhile, in Germany, an appalling decade of crisis and misery had finally brought to power the man who, in-directly, was perhaps the one factor that finally ended the depression – Hitler.

Clemenceau's demands from Germany had gravely im-poverished that country; in their hatred the French and the Germans had done each other irreparable mischief. Im-patient of receiving their reparations, the French had marched into the Ruhr in 1923 to take them by force by running the industries themselves. But the Germans had refused to co-operate and the whole industrial system had come to a halt; in the ensuing months the German currency had been wrecked.

The mark, which fell from 4·20 to the dollar to 7,000 in 1922, fell in 1923 to 160,000 in July, to 242,000 in

October and to the unbelievable figure of 4,200,000,000 in November. And as the mark fell the printing presses tried to keep pace. Prices soared even while the customers

"PHEW! THAT'S A NASTY LEAK, THANK GOODNESS IT'S NOT AT OUR END OF THE BOAT."

May 24, 1932

An early version of "I'm all right Jack." Although the slump was world-wide governments did little collectively to help overcome it. Low brilliantly showed how Britain, France and the U.S. failed to recognise that recovery was made harder by their not helping Middle-European countries where the crisis was even more severe.

waited and millions of marks were required to buy a pound of butter. It became impossible to do business and barter replaced ordinary monetary payments. There were food riots and despair; fortunes and savings accumulated by laborious efforts over the years vanished in a night.

Germany had never recovered. By 1933 unemployment was enormous and the country was seething with unrest. The Communists, many of whom had filtered across the Russian border and started the revolution in Kiel that overthrew the Kaiser in 1918, had gained ground — in spite of private armies raised against them and the political terrorism that resulted.

Hitler, an impassioned demagogic orator, provoked and played on latent anti-semitic and anti-Marxist sentiments in Germany, persuading people that a Jewish and Communist group was responsible for Germany's weakness. Within a few years the German Worker's Party, of which he had been an insignificant member, had become the National Socialist or Nazi Party, with Hitler's nationalist and anti-Marxist creed as its programme.

His attempt to make the German war general, Ludendorff, a dictator had resulted only in his own imprisonment, but by 1930 he was the unchallenged head of a powerful party pledged to put Germany back on her feet. Industrialists, afraid of a Communist take-over of their plants, and senior officers, seeing in him the means of rebuilding their dismembered forces, gave him their support. When the world economic upheaval came in the early thirties, the Nazis exploited the disillusioned and discontented as well as the more solid middle classes who saw their standard of living threatened by the crisis. In January 1933, with the aid of propaganda and trickery, Hitler was appointed Chancellor of the Third Reich.

Clemenceau's wheel had turned full circle. The very conditions which he had designed to destroy Germany were building up to destroy France. Hitler never attempted to hide the fact that it was his intention to regain the lost territories — if necessary by force.

* * *

But although the advent to power of Hitler in Germany, and Roosevelt with his suspect New Deal in America two months later, made foreigners believe that Britain was the only safe repository for their funds, unimaginative politicians at home, without the verve of Roosevelt or the ruthlessness of Hitler, allowed the depression in England to continue.

In the years immediately after the First World War, ex-Servicemen had taken to wearing their medals and parading with collecting boxes in the shopping areas. On Armistice Day, 1922, after the official procession had passed the Cenotaph in London, 25,000 unemployed men followed, wearing medals and pawn tickets and bearing on their banner the words, "From the living victims – the unemployed – to our own dead comrades who died in vain." In the years that followed, many more of these processions – usually from the North to London – were organised in a pathetic attempt to bring the plight of the unemployed home to their fellow-countrymen. Demonstrations and meetings were frequent, but the hopelessness of the unemployed was probably the reason for the comparative absence of violence.

By 1932, however, there was at last some sympathy for the unemployed. Many private charitable schemes were launched, and distressed towns were "adopted" by others more lucky. Jarrow, for instance, one of the hardest hit, was adopted by the county of Surrey. The sympathy was given public expression by the Duke of Windsor, then the Prince of Wales, at a public meeting at the Albert Hall, and by Dr. William Temple, then Archbishop of York, who urged that all Christians should support the restoration of the cuts in the unemployment benefits. By 1933 they were 25s. 3d. for a man with a wife and child.

Under pressure from public opinion, the weekly insurance payments were raised again in 1934, but only by a few pence, and they were never quite adequate. Inevitably some desperate men were driven to desperate expedients.

The National Unemployed Workers' Movement had been organised several years before by the Communist Party and many people believed incorrectly that it was financed by support from Moscow. It was immediately successful in attracting members, and while the Communist Party itself in England numbered only 5,000 at this period, the Unemployed Workers' Movement soon had more than 100,000. The entry fee was twopence and the subscription a penny a week. The collecting boxes disappeared from the streets and the hunger marches began as the only means of non-violent protest against the plight of the unemployed that was allowed by the police.

Thousands of unemployed men marched across the country in the next few years. They were selected for their strength and good health, and they marched in winter because it was felt that a march in sunny weather would not have the same emotional appeal. Some of the men collapsed en route because they had lived too long on fish and chips — and more often on chips alone — and on bread, with only occasional jam and margarine. For most of them, fresh milk had long since become a week-end luxury and fruit and greens a rare treat. Although they never actually starved, many were suffering from malnutrition.

But the marches went on. The marchers aimed at up to thirty miles a day, arranging their route so that they were able to stop at a town at night, where the local Labour Party would have arranged accommodation and a meal in some church hall.

The marches did a great deal towards rousing a sense of responsibilty in the country towards the unemployed. Hundreds of towns were passed through en route for London, and in each one a demonstration was held. Miners would carry their lamps and would light them as they arrived in a town at dusk, and the long lines of lamps swinging in the darkness had a deeply moving effect on the crowds lining the pavements to watch the men pass by.

The greatest of these marches, from Jarrow, took place in 1936. By then the slump was beginning to show signs of receding, but there were still over a million unemployed, most of them in the North. The Jarrow March has become a symbol of the Depression and was as much a milestone in British working-class history as the story of the Tolpuddle Martyrs.

In Victorian times, Jarrow, the home of the Venerable Bede, had developed rich coal, steel and shipbuilding industries, and although by the twentieth century coal and steel had declined, the principal Jarrow shipyard, Palmers', still employed 8,000 men out of a population of 37,000. Many of these men, believing that they were entering a new era of shared responsibility and profits, had actually put their savings into Palmers' when shares were offered to them in 1920. £76,000 of their money was invested.

Then with the depression, the bottom fell out of their lives. What happened in Jarrow was typical of what was happening all over industrial Britain. New methods of mass production were demanding larger industrial units. To assist themselves to modernise, under Norman's rationalisation plans, firms had for some time been organising themselves into combines so that they could afford new scientific developments and new plant. The Government themselves favoured industrial combination on the sensible grounds that only in this way could American competition be met, but it did mean that a great deal of power was concentrated in the hands of a small body of tycoons, and much bitterness was caused when manufacturers' associations began to buy up factories only to close them down. In fact, the goods produced in such factories were most likely no longer being produced economically and, in the face of foreign competition, the country could not support them. But there was inevitable suffering and large sections of the country became classed as "Distressed Areas". Jarrow was one such area.

While the country generally was improving, Jarrow had become one of the hardest hit. Its shipyards had been closed, and the bosses had even brought in covenants that sterilised sites to prevent them being used again for forty years. Palmers' was among the yards which had been sold out, but the money paid for it went not to the men who had held the shares but to the bank creditors. In 1934 the cranes were dismantled and the workshops were de-molished, and grass was allowed to grow on the site. In the words of Miss Ellen Wilkinson, Jarrow's first Labour M.P. — Red Ellen, as she was called — the town was being murdered.

Minister of Education in the Labour Government of 1945, Ellen Wilkinson, the daughter of a cotton worker, first went to Jarrow as its Member in 1935. She took it completely to her heart and represented it until her death in 1947. She had formerly represented Middlesbrough East until she lost her seat in the Labour débâcle of 1931, and there she had thought she had known what poverty meant. "But compared to Jarrow," she said, "things on the Tees-side were moving. Jarrow was utterly stagnant . . . No one had a job, except a few railwaymen, officials, the workers in the co-operative stores, and the few clerks and craftsmen who went out of the town to their jobs each day. The unemployment rate was over 80 per cent."

One of her first acts was to take 300 people from her constituency to talk to MacDonald, while the Prime Minister was visiting his constituency at Seaham. He had refused to meet Tyneside M.P.s, but she persuaded him to see her and eight of the 300 who had marched nine miles in a gale. He promised special consideration, but nothing was done. Later, another deputation saw Walter Runciman, then President of the Board of Trade, after a projected plan for a steelworks at Jarrow had been abandoned by the Iron and Steel Federation with the Government's approval. This meeting was equally abortive. "Jarrow," Runciman told them with icy indifference, "must work out its own salvation." This was the background to the march which became known as the Jarrow Crusade.

Runciman's imprudent remark caused furious resentment in men who wanted nothing more than to work out their own salvation. Someone suggested that unemployed men from Jarrow should march to London, telling people on the way of the callous treatment they had received. The march was supported by the Town Council and backed by the whole of Tyneside. About £800 was raised by appeal, and of this £1 a head was kept for the return fare by train. With the rest of the money, the committee bought leather and nails for the 200 men chosen, so they could mend their own boots, and waterproof groundsheets to be used as capes in wet weather. Field kitchens were lent by the Boy Scouts and a second-hand bus was bought to carry the men's kit and blankets. Prayers were said in every church and chapel in Jarrow and, on October 4th, 1936, the march began. A brass band played the men over the borough boundary and that night they slept at Chester-le-Street.

According to Ellen Wilkinson, who walked with the men, the march was never Communist-inspired and, though she consulted Communists who had organised other marches, she was wise enough to keep her march well clear of their control. There was certainly, however, Communist inspiration behind other marches that were converging on London and the party adroitly stressed its own part in the Jarrow March.

In fact, only two Communists took part in the Jarrow March, and the men were wholly law-abiding and always warmly received. At each stopping-place, those marchers who had Conservative sympathies called at the local Conservative Association's offices to explain their unhappy town's plight.

It was a courageous affair and much more lively than the other marches because of the pride of the Jarrow men. Newspapermen covering the affair gave mouth organs to the marchers to keep up their spirits, and in many towns en route people of all political persuasions contributed money and food. Crowds cheered as they went by and listened at their meetings.

Sometimes they arrived to beautifully set tables and bright lights, and immediately the men smartened up. But in other towns, mercifully few, they were treated like outcasts and the tables were bare boards and tea was poured into their mugs from buckets. On these occasions the men looked what they were — dependents on public assistance — and seemed, as Ellen Wilkinson said, "as grubby as their angry M.P." One contingent, preparing to march through York, for instance, found a police cordon across its path. The marchers were put up at a nearby workhouse and given only bread and margarine to eat while 200 police kept watch on them. This was exceptional, however, and almost everywhere else people were friendly.

A group of young doctors and medical students looked after the men on the way and improvised a clinic each evening, demanding no payment in return. Ellen Wilkinson — still weary herself — cut away socks that had become

H

embedded in broken blisters and bandaged the feet of men who had walked in agony. The march was a severe strain on men who had been undernourished for years.

The march took a little more than a month, but before they had been on the road more than a week, the Government — under the Conservative Baldwin since the retirement of MacDonald in 1935 — issued a statement saying that such marches were undesirable and that no deputation from them would be received. Even the T.U.C. and the Labour Party frowned on the march as likely to destroy sympathy with the workers' cause.

On arrival in London, there was a mass meeting in Hyde Park. It was organised by the Communist Party, though Clement Attlee, who was to become Prime Minister in 1945, was among the speakers. Thousands of people turned out to greet the men, banners were waved and songs were sung, but the actual results were meagre.

In fact a deputation was officially received and the Minister of Labour, Ernest Brown, was given an uncomfortable hour as he listened to the marchers' pleas. But the presentation of the Jarrow petition was only a gesture. One result was that Jarrow did get a certain amount of help from a new tube works that was started. But the Government on the whole showed indifference. All the Jarrow men had done, in fact, was tell the world of their plight. They could do no more.

*   *   *

The hunger marches were peaceful affairs, but there were some to whom protest was a more virile business, who felt that only a strong ruthless Government could answer the country's ills, and who were determined to try to provide one, however violent the consequences.

For years, taking its line from Mussolini, the Italian dictator, there had been a Fascist Party of sorts in England as indeed there was in most countries at that time. But it had remained the playground of retired officers and eccentric reactionaries and was treated with contempt until the arrival of Sir Oswald Mosley, a man who turned the derision into an undercurrent of fear.

A baronet, educated at Winchester and Sandhurst, Mosley had energy, intelligence, courage, oratorical power, money and an acceptable social position. He had begun his political career as a Conservative, but had later joined the Labour Party and been given a minor office in MacDonald's second Government. He had resigned in disgust, however, and in 1931 formed what was known as the New Party, from which he moved to the leadership of the British Union of Fascists. Under the slogan of "Action" and with its mocking references to politicians of all parties as "The Old Gang" and "The Ostrich Brigade", the B.U.F. declared itself the party of youth and claimed to stand for virile government, without, however, stating how this was to be carried out.

The kind of oratory that Mosley offered, as with Hitler's in Germany, at first attracted some idealists, though they did not stay in the movement long. But throughout 1933 new members poured in at an impressive rate. By 1934 there were said to be 400 branches and a total membership of 20,000.

Mosley had carefully studied the Fascist movements abroad and he copied them slavishly, even to the black shirts from which the Fascists got their name, and the floodlit meetings and the salutes and the cries of "Hail Mosley!" This kind of crude demagogy alienated many people who might otherwise have sympathised. Had Mosley been more politically shrewd and less anxious for results, he might well have evolved an esentially English form of Fascism which could have been much more dangerous.

Nevertheless, by 1936 the Fascists felt strong enough to provoke violence by organised marches through the East End of London, for years the acknowledged stamping ground of the Communists.

"A large van," one description runs, "looking like a police van, which was in itself irritating, arrived on the scene with a spotlight, and in due course there marched on the scene the military organisation of the Blackshirts. The next thing that happened was that a body of police arrived, and there was a feeling going right through the East End that somehow or other the police were in sympathy."

Certainly the police seemed to be protecting the Fascists. In October 1936, for instance, a march from the Royal Mint to Whitechapel provoked crowded streets. The police cordoned them off and made way for the Fascists, who came up in their usual closed vehicles. More than a dozen wireless vans were used to control the crowds and aircraft were used for reconnaissance. In an attempt to clear the road, police carrying batons made charges in Cable Street where the infuriated crowd had torn up paving stones and built barricades. There was hand-to-hand fighting, chiefly between the police and the Communist and Socialist demonstrators, many of whom were arrested.

On Mosley's arrival, a forest of Union Jacks on decorated poles rose into the air. More unsuccessful attempts were made to disperse the crowds and finally the march to Whitechapel was called off. Instead, the Fascists marched, heavily escorted by police, westwards to the Embankment and Trafalgar Square. As they went they pasted labels —

"Every Jew is a Burden on the Back of a Gentile" and "Kill the Dirty Jews" — to hoardings.

The complaints of the public, curiously, were not so much about the Fascists' behaviour as of police brutality, though hecklers at Fascist meetings were usually given the notorious knuckle-duster treatment of Hitler's thugs.

A meeting they held at the Albert Hall was typical of other meetings held in provincial cities. There was the usual sickening spectacle of flags, spotlights, drums and bugles that Europe had grown so used to, and the police packed the entire front of the building to make sure the hecklers could not reach the platform. A huge crowd milled outside and the police had to smuggle late-arriving Fascists into the hall.

The mounted police, attempting to drive a crowd of 3,000 down Exhibition Road, found their difficulties increased by the traffic which was at a standstill for half a mile in every direction. Again many demonstrators were arrested and, as on other occasions, there were protestations of police brutality and of their partiality towards the Fascists.

"I could not help shuddering," Geoffrey Lloyd, Baldwin's Parliamentary Private Secretary and an eye-witness at an earlier meeting said, "at the thought of this vile bitterness copied from foreign lands being brought into the centre of England."

The Government was slow to act against the Fascists but eventually the danger of rioting and bloodshed led in 1937 to their introducing the Public Order Act, which banned the wearing of political uniforms. There was one last defiant march that October with the usual clashes, but with the new Act, a blanket descended on the Fascist movement. While the Nazi Party was holding Germany to ransom by terror and brutality, the British Union of Fascists, deprived of its trappings, ignored by the Press and suffering from internal splits, quickly began to fade from the public eye. Besides, by this time, bigger things were in the air to attract attention. Quite clearly, a war was coming, and the contest no longer seemed to be one between Right and Left but between Hitler and the human race.

Fourteen / New Blood

As the thirties drew to a close, the depression was coming to an end. It had permeated the life of the country — *Love on the Dole* by Walter Greenwood had been a best-selling novel and later a play and a film, and *Brother, Can You Spare A Dime?* was a popular song of the period. Although things were improving in 1936, there were still 1,700,000 unemployed, and the Government still seemed to be fiddling with the problem.

Ramsay MacDonald had retired by this time to give way to Baldwin. He had reigned "in increasing decrepitude", as Churchill said, "at the summit of the British system, a man for whom the springs of action had broken". Even Snowden, his friend, had turned on him at last and in a typically waspish resignation speech had advised the Cabinet to "look into the case of the Prime Minister, not only in his own interests but in the interests of the country, for it is a positive danger that its affairs should be in the hands of a man who every time he speaks exposes his ignorance or incapacity". With his departure, government had appeared to have become a job for the boys, with the same old faces always in office.

The Prince of Wales, who had strong sympathy for the unemployed, tried to make contact with them in their homes, and helped to found clubs and social centres for them. But the Government, although it appointed Commissioners to deal with the problem, allowed them little funds and no powers, and the training centres and labour camps where men worked for 5s. 0d. a week pocket-money were denounced by the unemployed as "slave camps". Distressed areas became in turn "depressed areas" and later "special areas" — a fine point that may have given satisfaction

The Government after much thought having appointed a Commissioners to think about The Derelict Areas, is now about to think about what has been thought about them. —OFFICIAL.

THE THINKER.

September 19, 1934

The Depression produced endless Commissions and Reports, on which remarkably little action was taken. Even the men appointed to deal with the Depressed Areas were given little or no power. (Stanley Baldwin as Rodin's statue.)

in Whitehall, but precious little in Jarrow and Rotherham and the Rhondda where, in 1936, over a quarter of the unemployed had on average been out of work for no less than fifty-six months.

The trouble in these areas was that so little money was in circulation. Towns that had been dependent on a single depressed industry needed, as Keynes had always insisted, an injection of completely new blood in the form of alternative industries to start the money moving again. But nothing

was done. Chancellors of the Exchequer — even Snowden —
believed that taxation of wealth was at saturation point and
governmental policies kept capital tied down.

In the words of one of Priestley's characters, the game was
"slowing up. Like playing poker with chips made of melting
ice".

It was not until 1937, that the idea of relocating industries began to be seriously considered. Although the
Government had brought in various measures to encourage
economic revival such as tariffs and aid to agriculture and
shipping, these did nothing directly to decrease unemployment.

One natural remedy for the depressed areas, of course, was
to shift the population and, aided by grants from the
Ministry of Labour, many left their homes and moved to
London and the south-east where the unemployment rate
was not much more than half the national average. The
population of South Wales fell by 115,000 (or 6 per cent)
between 1931 and 1938, and Northumberland and Durham
by 39,000. Nevertheless, this only touched on the problem
and the Commissioners demanded more powers and more
money. Grants were therefore made through them to
private firms to assist them to start new industries in the
badly-hit areas and help was also given by organisations
such as the Special Areas Reconstruction Association and the
Nuffield Trust.

Meanwhile the Treasury had made loans to assist the
building of what became known as trading estates, sites
already equipped with factories to rent. These estates were
the idea of a man called S. A. Sadler Forster, a Middlesbrough accountant who was secretary of the Tees-side
Development Committee. The Government, he claimed,
should back these estates with subsidies to tempt new light

industries to the distressed areas. The Times took up the idea in its leader columns and, in what was conceivably an attempt to gain votes just before the 1935 election, the Cabinet agreed to provide £2,000,000 to construct the first of such estates in the north-east of England. Sadler Forster was appointed chairman of the scheme.

The site was a stretch of valueless land on the outskirts of Gateshead which had to be levelled and covered with pit slag. In June, 1937, hundreds of shabby men appeared on it with picks, shovels and barrows — the unemployed from Gateshead, Jarrow and the Shields. The hard labour almost killed many of them for whom it was the first real work they had for a decade. And apart from the blisters and backaches, they were sceptical about the whole enterprise. Light industry, where a man's strength didn't count, seemed a poor sort of job compared with steel, mining or shipbuilding.

Nevertheless, there was money to be earned and they were glad of the work, and the factories went up, to be advertised at staggeringly cheap rates — a complete factory for a pound a week including rates. When the estate was finished everyone sat back and waited for the miracle. Not one request was received.

It was a dreadful shock. It seemed as though the whole scheme was hopeless after all. But help came unexpectedly from another quarter. A few Jewish manufacturers, driven from Germany by Hitler, saw in the estate their only hope of starting in business again. They had had to leave their capital behind and they could afford very little, but they still had their skills, and factories at a pound a week seemed like a gift from heaven. Their example, and further advertising, finally aroused the interest of British manufacturers, and by 1939 there were 5,000 people working on the estate.

In fact, however, such projects barely touched the problem of the hundreds of thousands of men employed in the basic industries of coal, iron and steel, shipbuilding and textiles. It was Hitler who was to be their salvation.

From the start Hitler had made plain his determination to bring about the economic and military recovery of Germany — no matter by what means. It was soon clear that this included the acquisition of what he called lebensraum, or living space, for the cramped millions of his country, even if he had to take back by force those areas which had been lost at Versailles. Gradually, under the cover of glider and sailing clubs and youth movements, he had rebuilt the German army, navy and air force. He had repudiated the Versailles Treaty and taken back the Saar and the Rhineland and, in 1936, his confident troops were fighting in the Spanish Civil War, the "armed rehearsal" for the greater conflict of 1939, which drew so many left-wing idealists into the fray.

The politicians of the twenties and thirties, believing that the 1914–18 war had been "the war to end war", had allowed Britain's forces to be sadly run down, and Baldwin had for years resisted rearmament. But he, too, at last acknowledged that Britain was in danger of being overwhelmed by the very nation she had helped to bring to its knees only twenty years before. In 1937, the British Government embarked on a £1,500,000,000 rearmament programme.

With that decision, to all intents and purposes, the depression was over. Arms contracts were directed to the special areas where new works began to be built. A solution to the unemployment problem had turned up at last, though the Government had been driven to it less by compassion for the men out of work than by fear of aggression.

It was almost too late. By this time there were 80,000 men
over 45 who, in the words of a report by the Commissioners
for the Special Areas, "had become practically a standing
army of unemployed", and worse still, there were too large
a number of young men who were "content to live in idleness as State pensioners" and were unwilling to make any
effort to find work. "They had grown up in an atmosphere
of idleness", and were in fact, "demoralised by the seeming
inevitableness of unemployment".

Nevertheless, at last the heavy industries got going again
—not easily because so many of the men had lost their
skills. The furnaces were started up once more and ships
reappeared on the slipways, to follow to the sea the giant
Cunarder, Queen Mary, which had been laid down in 1932
and remained on the slip until 1934, a constant reminder of
the depression. And when it was all totted up, it was found
to the amazement of those experts who had prophesied
disaster, that the heavy cost of the rearmament was, in fact,
no burden at all.

For years everyone had been preaching retrenchment and
making cuts to save money, convinced it was the only way
to keep the economy alive. But with the cuts, and the men
thrown out of work, the country's spending power had
dried up, and as it had disappeared more cuts had been
made and the spending power had declined further, so that
it became rather like treating a case of anaemia with leeches.

The rearmament programme when it came was like a
shot in the arm. The saving on the unemployment benefits
as men left the dole at long last and the increased spending
power of those who were working once more put money on
the move again. In a very short time, the cost of the new
weapons was cancelled out.

Norman's policies were renounced at last. Although he

remained as a despot at the Bank of England until 1944, outside the Bank his power was ended and people at last began to listen to Keynes. In 1936, Keynes had set out his

"GAD, SIR, AT ANY RATE WE ARE RESTORING PROSPERITY."

July 10, 1935

Although the Labour Party, to which most of the unemployed belonged, was against rearmament, the unpalatable fact remained that rearmament was the one thing that started industry moving again and gave the unemployed back their jobs. (The figure in the bath-towel is Colonel Blimp, the character whom Low invented to ridicule contemporary clap-trap, particularly from the Old Tories.)

beliefs in a book, The General Theory of Employment, Interest and Money, which was transforming the economic thinking in Great Britain and was to establish him beyond argument as the world's leading economist.

But for a few stubborn and short-sighted men, might the problem have been solved a decade earlier?

Fifteen / Can It Happen Again?

THE revival was slow but by the end of the thirties every-one knew that things were changing. It wasn't just that a war was approaching — and everyone knew that well enough as fighting ground to a halt in Spain and the demands of the confident dictators grew louder — it was that a whole wretched way of life was coming to an end, a way of life in which misery had eaten away generosity and idealism, and when, in the general *sauve qui peut*, men had become cynical and hard.

The activities of the National Workers' Movement had not ceased, however, and as late as December 1938, forty unemployed men stopped the traffic in Oxford Circus by lying down in the roadway. As fast as the police picked them up, others took their place and the traffic came to a halt for the best part of an hour. On the following day, fifty more of them marched into the Ritz and asked for tea, and on Boxing Day, another group sang mock carols outside the home of the Chairman of the Unemployment Assistance Board, while on New Year's Eve twelve more climbed the Monument and hung out a banner demanding winter relief. On the same day, hundreds more carried a plain black coffin, marked "He did not get winter relief" down the Strand to Piccadilly. Police charges dispersed them.

Two or three days later, however, the coffin turned up in Downing Street in a lorry. The demonstrators wished to present it to the new Prime Minister, Neville Chamberlain, who had succeeded to the Conservative Party on Baldwin's retirement. But the police were expecting them and there was a ridiculous shoving match between the men trying to get the coffin over the tailboard and the police trying to push it back. A week later in Glasgow a flag was seen flying over the Unemployment Assistance Board office, "This is the office . . . which starves men, women and children", and not long afterwards men chained themselves to the railings outside Labour Exchanges carrying placards, "Release Us From Hunger". In 1939, a shabby group demanding jobs burst in among the boiled shirts and white ties at a dinner attended by Sir John Anderson, head of Air Raid Precautions, and even in the summer of 1940, with the war threatening to overwhelm Britain, there were still 1,000,000 unemployed.

Everybody who had any conscience at all, however, had by this time given their sympathies wholeheartedly to the workless. The awareness of the nation was stirred. Young men of good family who in the twenties would have been willing to break the General Strike for a "lark" had begun to turn seriously to the Left. They helped the marches and joined the Communist Party and the Labour Party in a tremendous swing that swept Attlee to power in 1945.

The war had saved us. In 1945 the unemployed numbered only just over 100,000 and never since, until the present day, have there been anything like half a million unemployed.

It was over, leaving its scars and its heartbreak, and in the minds of the older men the constant question, "Can it happen again?"

Further Reading

For those who wish to know more about the depression, the files of any newspaper of the period will tell the story, but the following books, which I myself have used, are also worth reading:

The British Economy, 1920–1957, A. J. Youngson (Unwin University Books, 1960)

The Baldwin Age, ed. John Raymond (Eyre and Spottiswoode, 1960)

The Thirties, Julian Symons (Cresset Press, 1960)

The Town That Was Murdered, Ellen Wilkinson (Gollancz, 1939)

The Mutiny At Invergordon, Kenneth Edwards (Putnam, 1937)

A Pattern of Rulers, Francis Williams (Longmans, 1965)

Great Britain, 1886–1935, J. A. Spender (Cassell, 1936)

Issues In American Economic History, ed. G. D. Nash (Heath, 1964)

Novels which reflect the period include the works of George Orwell and the books of northern authors like J. B. Priestley, who saw it all at first hand.